MW00588259

★★★★ At the ★★★★
Apple's Core
THE BEATLES FROM THE INSIDE

★★★★ At the ★★★★
Apple's Core
THE BEATLES FROM THE INSIDE

Denis O'Dell
with Bob Neaverson

PETER OWEN
London

PETER OWEN LTD
73 Kenway Road, London SW5 0RE

First published in Great Britain 2002
by Peter Owen Publishers

© Denis O'Dell and Bob Neaverson, 2002

All rights reserved.
No part of this publication may be reproduced in any form
or by any means without the prior permission of the publishers.

A catalogue record for this book is available from
the British Library

ISBN 0 7206 1116 4

Printed and bound in India
by Thomson Press Ltd

To Donna, for keeping me sane through the Beatle years
– D.O'D.

And with thanks to Bodil for all her support
– B.N.

Foreword by Martin Lewis

NUMEROUS FACTORS LED to the stratospheric success of the Beatles in the 1960s and have contributed to the unparalleled situation in which their popularity is undiminished over thirty years after their disbandment.

One of the less celebrated facets is the quality of the creative and business associates that a mixture of providence and savvy instinct brought into their tight inner circle. This book by Denis O'Dell is a very important attestation to that aspect of the Beatles' kingdom.

Broadly speaking, there were two strands of people who entered the Beatles' professional world. There were those who caught the Beatle bus early on and became loyal courtiers for all (or most of) the ride; and those who were recruited for specific projects.

The first category includes their manager Brian Epstein (wilfully undersung in recent years), their record producer George Martin and their most effective publicist/propaganda minister Derek Taylor. These comprised the Three Wise Men at the core of the Beatles' evolution from young hopefuls in a Liverpool manger to becoming the Supreme Beings of popular culture in the twentieth century. Also in this inner circle were their stalwart road managers Neil Aspinall and Mal Evans and ever-loyal 'Mr Fix-It' Alistair Taylor. And, although his subsequent actions betrayed his ultimate loyalty, their music publisher Dick James was also an intimate.

In the second category come people such as movie producer Walter Shenson and film director Richard Lester – the team that made *A Hard*

Day's Night and *Help!* – and director Michael Lindsay-Hogg who directed their early promotional films and their cinematic swansong *Let It Be*. Photographer/designer Robert Freeman, who enshrined their evolving visual image on five successive album covers, is another. If you proved effective on one project the Beatles conferred their loyalty and brought you back for subsequent ventures.

Denis O'Dell, however, belongs in a category by himself. Although he entered the Beatles' universe much like Shenson and Lester – a hired hand to work on a specific production – such was the respect and comfort level he inspired in the Beatles that he was subsequently invited to join their team in a different capacity. And that was a rarity.

In full disclosure, I should state that I have had the honour of friendship with many of the folks mentioned above and have worked with several of them on other post-Beatles endeavours. Indeed Derek Taylor was my first boss and became my mentor. My views therefore are hardly devoid of partisan loyalty. But I believe that my familiarity with so many of those in the inner circle has given me insights into the truly effective members of the Beatles' 'kitchen cabinet'. And Denis certainly is in that bracket.

The late Walter Shenson was an astute and entrepreneurial producer – superb at the big picture and unerring in making instinctive choices. But he had entered the film world as a publicist and did not have the experience or interest in the extensive hands-on detail that is essential in day-to-day film production. To get *A Hard Day's Night* made on a minuscule budget and with a tight schedule – not to mention the problems caused by the the whole of Britain being in the throes of Beatlemania – was a monumental organizational task. There is no shadow of doubt that Denis's intensive production work on the film was a major factor in its successful completion. In producing the DVD edition of the film recently I interviewed numerous members of the crew and cast who testified to the crucial role he played.

His indefatigable spirit and can-do philosophy clearly made a marked impression on the Beatles. For, while a prior commitment precluded his involvement on the *Help!* movie, when in 1967 the Beatles formulated their plans for Apple and foresaw the need for a film division it was to Denis that they turned. They had recognized in him a kindred soul with his swashbuckling approach to solving problems and making things happen; the very opposite of the 'business as usual' attitude that was such anathema to the Beatles.

In the gloriously idealistic and chaotic madness that was Apple there were idealists and pragmatists. Denis was in the latter category, and his calm manner and astute instincts were much valued in the overall company – not just the film division. That Apple didn't realize its full potential was a result of the well-documented fragmentation in the personal relationships among its four owners.

Denis's insights into that aspect of the Beatles' story are a marvellous addition to our understanding of that era. *At the Apple's Core* is an essential book for any Beatles fan or student, offering a rare glimpse into the inner life of the Fab Four by one of The Few – a trusted member of the inner circle.

Denis refers in his book to the symbiotic relationship between the individual members of the Beatles and Monty Python which developed from chance late-sixties encounters, such as Ringo appearing in Denis's film production *The Magic Christian* – co-written by John Cleese and Graham Chapman – to full-blown late-seventies endeavours, such as George financing the Python's *Life of Brian* and his cameo appearance in the affectionate Beatles spoof documentary *The Rutles*, created by Neil Innes and Eric Idle.

That blossoming relationship between the two groups who broke all the rules in their respective worlds of music and comedy led to one misconception that has long been a mild irritation to Denis. When George Harrison formed his HandMade Films production company in October 1978, he took as his business partner a soft-spoken American wheeler-dealer named Denis O'Brien – a name that at casual glance was very reminiscent of the Denis O'Dell who had worked in film with the Beatles. And that similarity led to situations where people confused 'Denis O'B' and 'Denis O'D'. After all, both were in the film business and had a Beatles connection.

After HandMade Films contributed to the revival of the British film industry in the eighties and became a very profitable company, George Harrison undertook an audit of his company's accounts and discovered to his horror that his business partner had apparently embezzled over $25 million. A court case was pursued and on 10 January 1996 a Los Angeles judge found in George's favour and demanded that O,'Brien return $11.6 million of the embezzled funds. Despite the judgement and much effort, to this date none of the money has been returned.

Some of the Python members (notably the late Graham Chapman) had seen through O'Brien's skilful act in the earliest days of his appearance on the Python scene. Others – most regrettably George Harrison – took longer to discover O'Brien's true colours.

Having produced several stage shows and films with Python members between 1976 and 1982 as benefits for Amnesty International, I had become familiar with O'Brien and shared Chapman's jaundiced view of his smooth patter. I vividly remember an occasion in 1980 in which John Cleese (with whom I worked closely on all the 'Secret Policeman's Ball' productions) telephoned me. Apparently on the receiving end of a pitch from Denis O'Brien – and vaguely convinced that his credentials were immaculate because of his work with the Beatles – he said: 'Martin, I'm confused. Who is Denis O'Dell and who is Denis O'Brien – and what's the difference between them?' I recall telling him: 'Easy. Denis O'Dell worked with the Beatles and was very effective for them in the film world. And Denis O'Brien is Allen Klein in sheep's clothing!' John thanked me for this insight but – perhaps not getting my drift – continued to be involved in a couple of O'Brien productions. One hopes he got paid . . . In any event, there should be no more confusion. It is Denis O' Dell and only Denis O'Dell who was the Beatles' man of film!

No words about Denis can conclude without a mention of his unique place in Beatles' history and folklore – his name being enshrined in a Beatles song! It is true that Brian's former assistant Peter Brown is mentioned in passing in the 'Ballad of John and Yoko' in his functionary role as a conveyer of information regarding the marital rules of Gibraltar, while John's 'Give Peace a Chance' referenced Derek Taylor (neatly rhymed with Norman Mailer!), and an early (discarded) version of George's solo track 'The Art of Dying' included a reference to 'Mr Epstein'. But none of those compare with John's affectionate throwaway references to 'Denis O'Bell' (just one consonant away from Denis's actual name) on the Beatles' 'You Know My Name (Look Up the Number)'.

Why did John use Denis's name in that song? While John never explained it publicly the answer is obvious. That song was a rare comedic gem from the lads who were simply having fun in the studio. In the style of the ditties they created for their legendary Christmas records for fan-club members, it was reminiscent of their love of the silliness of the *Goon Show* (the fifties radio precursor to Monty Python). And in that relaxed mode, when John thought that it would be fun to give name to a lounge singer of this goofy chanson he instinctively threw in a variant of the name of a good chum. There are few higher honours than to have been a chum of the Beatles. So let's hear it for Denis O'Dell . . .

Martin Lewis
Beatles historian and producer of the DVD edition of
A Hard Day's Night

Preface

My involvement with the Beatles represents just a small fraction of my life and career. Before I met them on the set of their first film, *A Hard Day's Night*, I had, before and after leaving the RAF, worked on scores of British films as a writer, assistant director and associate producer. Inevitably, they represent a fairly mixed bag in terms of success and critical acclaim. Some, such as *Scrooge* (1951), *Tom Brown's Schooldays* (1951) and *The Pickwick Papers* (1952), have attained recognition in the annals of film history, while others, such as *Trottie True* (1949) and *Valley of the Eagles* (1951), have long since sunk into obscurity. After my time with the Beatles in the sixties I continued to work in the film industry, producing or associate-producing films such as *The Offence* (1973), *Royal Flash* (1975) and *Robin and Marian* (1976). I was also involved with the production of Michael Cimino's *Heaven's Gate*. In the seventies Sean Connery and I started a film company, Tantallon Productions.

This book discusses the Beatles years only. Fortunately, throughout most of my time at Apple, in 1968 and early 1969, I kept a diary of dates and appointments. I had to. The period I spent with the Beatles was probably the most frantic of my career and, because they preferred to record throughout the night, those of us who were involved in their business and creative lives were frequently forced to burn the candle at both ends. I often found myself working around the clock, and I'd be lying if I said that there were not times when it took its toll. Yet, although I have some regrets about what I was unable to achieve with the Beatles, there is little I would change about those years. It was extraordinary and exhilarating to be caught up in the whirlwind of social, creative and financial activity that being an Apple executive entailed.

So much was going on at Apple during that period and especially in relation to the band's personal and artistic development that it is difficult not to feel overawed. After all, 1968 alone saw the formation of Apple, the Beatles' infatuation with the Maharishi Mahesh Yogi, the production and release of *Yellow Submarine*, the recording of the so-called 'White Album', the release of the 'Lady Madonna' and 'Hey Jude' singles . . .

I could go on. But the point is, the sheer dynamism of the Beatles' career was such that it now seems impossible that they could have achieved so much in such a short time. Some thirty years later it feels almost unreal, as if somehow there must have been more days per annum. Or perhaps, as their cartoon counterparts suggested in *Yellow Submarine*, time went on strike.

I entered the film industry in 1939 and, the war years notwithstanding, spent my entire career in film production. Throughout, I worked with a great many stars and directors. Some, including Richard Attenborough, Sean Connery, Richard Harris and Sidney Poitier, are still with us. Many, such as Alec Guinness, Yul Brynner and Audrey Hepburn, sadly are not, and, although this book deals with a relatively short period of time, an unnerving number of the people that you will encounter in these pages are also gone, most recently, of course, George Harrison.

I was at my house in Almeria, Spain, when I heard the dreadful news of his death. I like to think of my Spanish place as a peaceful refuge and do not have a television there. I was alerted by a neighbour who saw the early morning reports and called me immediately. Of course, George's demise was no surprise. His illness had been widely discussed in the world's press, and some weeks earlier, at a private lunch at Apple, company head Neil Aspinall had confirmed the seriousness of his condition. But it still seems unbelievable that we exist in a world where only two of the Beatles live and breathe. At the lunch with Neil we were looking over some Beatles memorabilia, among them a 'team photo' of the original people at Apple from 1968. A palpable sense of loss descended momentarily as we realized that many of those in the picture were no longer with us. That sense of loss seems to pervade the Beatles' story in a way that is as tragic as their music is joyous. I'm not suggesting any ridiculous 'conspiracy' theories about this, but it must be said that many of the key players from different phases of the Beatles' lives seem to have died before their time. Among them are Julia Lennon, Mary McCartney, Stuart Sutcliffe, Brian Epstein, Mal Evans, John Lennon, Ron Kass, Maureen Starkey, Derek Taylor, Linda McCartney . . . and now George. It is almost impossible to discuss his death without the risk of sounding trite or insincere, and by the time you read this book you will have read a thousand tributes discussing his cultural importance, as a songwriter and musician, as a philanthropist and as one of the people who introduced world music to the West. He was, of course, all of these things and more, but now is not the time or place to recount them. Everybody, even those fans who never had the pleasure of knowing him personally, will have their own memories. I prefer to remember him as he first appeared to me, sitting on the train while we were shooting the first scenes of *A Hard Day's Night* in 1964, full of wit, energy and earnest charm, the energetic youth of the Beatles transmitting seductive glances to a beautiful blonde schoolgirl across the carriage. It all seems so very long ago.

Denis O'Dell

Contents

Illustrations

India, 1968, between page 160 and 161

Introduction

IN MID-1969 I went to the Beatles' Apple offices in Savile Row, London, to resign as a director of Apple Corps. The company had recently been taken over by a savvy New York accountant called Allen Klein. Under his management I couldn't envisage any active role for myself as a part of Apple and thought it best simply to leave and return to producing films. While I was there, Paul showed me the management contract that Klein wanted the Beatles to sign and told me that he had absolutely no intention of complying. It was clear that the Beatles' own relationships with each other were fast approaching termination, and I felt that my working relationship with them had run its course. This realization was not untainted by a certain sadness. My association with them did, after all, go back to 1964, and during that time I had shared a great deal of my working and personal life with them. By that point I had worked as Associate Producer on *A Hard Day's Night* and *How I Won the War*, produced *Magical Mystery Tour*, become one of the six original directors of Apple Corps, organized a number of promos for their singles, set up the production of *Let It Be* and produced *The Magic Christian*, which featured Ringo Starr and Peter Sellers.

During that time I witnessed the madness of Beatlemania from the inside and shared a number of experiences with them, some sad, some bizarre, some baffling and infuriating and many of them joyous and exhilarating. I helped them to establish their own business empire and, in the end, saw their financial, personal and artistic aspirations deteriorate beyond all recognition. *At The Apple's Core* is not – and does not aim to be – a definitive history of the Beatles' career or a detailed analysis of their business or artistic dealings (although you will find that these are often discussed). Rather, it is a personal account of my life with the Beatles between 1964 and 1970.

Ever since I met the Beatles I have been asked by journalists and writers to give interviews about my association with the group. I have usually refused because I do not like the idea of having the things you say taken out of context and twisted to fit the agenda of that particular writer's or publication's bias. That changed in March 1996 when I agreed to let Bob Neaverson interview me for a book he was writing called *The Beatles Movies*. We talked for many hours, and he suggested that I should write a book of my own about my time with the group. Half joking, I told him that if I liked his book then maybe we could work on something together. Three years later we agreed to do just that. That's *how* this book came into being. *Why* it came into being is another matter.

The main reason for my writing my account is that over the years I have become increasingly dismayed by a number of histories of the group that are inaccurate about the Beatles, Apple and my relation-ship with them. A mountain of Beatles books has been published over the past thirty-five years. A few, such as Ian MacDonald's *Revolution in the Head*, have been inspirational. Many, however, are not. One author, whose recent Beatles reference book purports to be the most comprehensive one on the group ever produced, has a short entry (consisting of three paragraphs) on me in which he says that I am Irish-born (I was born in London), that I worked on the film *The Family Way* (I didn't), that I was involved in the production of *The Concert for Bangladesh* (I wasn't) and that I went on to form Hand-made Films with George Harrison (I didn't; I suspect he has confused me with Denis O'Brien). If this author is, as the book's blurb claims, the 'world's leading authority' on the group I'd hate to meet his deputy!

Shoddy research over a few facts are inoffensive and sometimes quite amusing. However, when poor research or inaccurate information lead to defamatory remarks and claims, it's a different matter. I was extremely angered to be portrayed, as I was in Philip Norman's *Shout! The True Story of the Beatles*, as a kind of fat cat who was awarded a munificent salary and who was effectively kicked out of Apple by Allen Klein. There are two fundamental errors here. I was never awarded high-powered director's fees by the Beatles, and I was not removed by Klein. I cannot speak for the other Apple executives – and, sadly, Ron Kass can no longer speak for himself – but if there were any who squandered some of the Beatles' fortune on high living it's certainly something I never experienced.

I left Apple to produce *The Magic Christian*. When I returned, the acrimony within the group was such that I decided there was no point in staying. I had also by then heard disturbing rumours about Klein's business practices, but I left the organization of my own free will.

Over the years I have found it upsetting to have my association with the Beatles portrayed so inaccurately. And what is worrying from a historical perspective are the implications of this. Books on the Fab Four often sell in huge quantities. Presented as 'definitive', they are snapped up by Beatles fans and scholars who, for the most part, digest the material they contain in unquestioning good faith, believing the 'facts' they present to be accurate and carefully researched. Once published, the power of the printed word ensures that such misinformation becomes accepted truth and this, in turn, perpetuates further myths.

Part of the problem, I suspect, is rooted in the need to find a dramatic new angle or 'spin' on such a familiar story. It seems that these days an even-handed perspective often isn't enough, that only a muckraking exercise or some supreme character annihilation will do the job. In a cultural climate where 'substance' and 'balance' have become ever more subservient to 'concept' and 'angle', publishers have been ever more keen to compete for the most sensationalistic interpretations of the Beatles' lives they can get away with. And those books that demonize various members of the group are, depressingly, almost always the biggest sellers.

This sensationalism extends also to the perception of the Apple organization, which is usually presented as a terrible and unmitigated failure, a kind of latter-day 'Fall of the Roman Empire'. The usual line is that millions of pounds were blown on gargantuan parties or that the Beatles' fortune was drained from them by sycophantic journalists, opportunistic swindlers and other hangers-on. This isn't total fabrication, of course, but the problem is that our sound-bite culture seems ever more eager to accentuate the negative, and truth, or at least perspective, is often the first casualty. The fact that Apple today is one of the most successful entertainment companies in the world is a fact that most tabloid journalists prefer to forget.

Although it's unfashionable these days, I'm proud to be able to say that this book doesn't have an agenda beyond that of recounting my own experiences, opinions and perceptions. I have no axe to grind and no scores to settle. There is no angle or 'spin'. However, I hope that this book will set the record straight and that it will furnish your understanding of the Beatles' career with a new set of insights. But, most of all, I hope that this book will enhance the pleasure you take in their music and films by conveying some of the exhilaration they provided for me.

Unlike many commentators writing about the group today, I was privileged to know them well throughout the heady days of Beatlemania. Like the rest of us, they could be unpleasant, selfish and vindictive, but they were also charming, entertaining and capable of great acts of kindness, compassion and love. In short, they were human beings, a fact that our tabloid culture seems to have forgotten or suppressed in the quest for a good story. The Beatles were, as human beings go, pretty remarkable, too. As their story continues to dissolve into a haze of assumptions, suppositions and lies, we would do well to remember this. As my old friend Derek Taylor once said, they represent the 'twentieth century's greatest romance'. Enjoy this book!

PART 1
The Eye of the Hurricane

1

Meet the Beatles

IN DECEMBER 1963 I returned to my house in St George's Square, London, from an exhausting stint in what was then Yugoslavia on a film adaptation of the Viking saga *The Long Ships*. The production, which starred Richard Widmark and Sidney Poitier, had been a difficult one. I was pretty tired and hoping for a rest when Bud Ornstein, head of the European branch of United Artists films, called me two days after I got home with an offer to associate-produce a low-budget musical, as yet untitled, starring a pop group from Liverpool called the Beatles. Having been out of England for some considerable time I was one of a very small minority who was unfamiliar with the Beatles. I had heard of them of course, but I had been abroad much of the year and had missed the phenomenal rise in popularity that had coincided with the release of their first and second successive British number one singles 'From Me to You' and 'She Loves You'. So I thanked Bud and told him that I would have to decline his offer as I needed a break.

If it had not been for a tiny twist of fate, that would have been the beginning, middle and end of my association with the Beatles. By pure chance, the phone call happened to come at a weekend when my teenage children, Denise, Shaun and Kevan, were visiting from the country. When they heard that I had turned down a film starring the Beatles they went berserk. They simply could not believe that I had just turned down the opportunity to work with their idols. I was simultaneously shocked and fascinated by their reaction. Their adulation of this group seemed to go far beyond that accorded to other musicians, and it was unusual for a pop act to appeal both to boys and girls equally. It wasn't long before I realized that it wasn't just my own children that were crazy about the group. During the summer of 1963 the Beatles had captured the collective imagination of British teenagers with a ferocity that was completely unprecedented. Kids didn't just like the Beatles. They *loved* them.

So appalled were my children at my gaffe that I felt compelled to call Bud back and accept the offer, on condition that I could leave straight away after the six weeks' shooting. Bud told me that would be fine. His main concern was to get the film made as cheaply and as quickly as possible, since pop groups' popularity rarely lasted more than about three months and United Artists didn't want to be lumbered with a movie featuring yesterday's men. At the time this made good sense. With the possible exception of Cliff Richard's films, British pop musicals were low-budget affairs, the common wisdom being that you made them as cheaply and quickly as possible and hoped to get them into the film theatres before the stars passed their sell-by dates. It was logical enough from a distributor's perspective, and for every half-decent sixties pop movie there are a hundred stinkers that now have nothing but kitsch appeal to recommend them. Admittedly this can be a draw, as anybody who has seen *Gonks Go Beat* will testify, but most have quite fairly been consigned to the dustbin of film history. Does anyone remember *The Ghost Goes Gear*? What about *Cuckoo Patrol*? If you do, you have my sincere sympathies. You are either a former member of Freddie and the Dreamers or you don't get out often enough!

The fact that I was to be working with the Beatles encouraged me to listen to their music. In fact, I considered it a necessity to find out as much as I could about them. It wasn't exactly difficult. Although my children had copies of the Beatles' singles, after agreeing to work on the picture I went out and bought the LP *Please Please Me*. Later, just before we started shooting, I acquired a copy of *With the Beatles*. Although a fan of Buddy Holly and Elvis, I was not particularly keen on British rock and roll and regarded singers such as Cliff Richard and Adam Faith as rather weak home-grown imitations of their American counterparts.

But the Beatles were a revelation to me. I was immediately struck, like millions of others, by their originality and musicality. It was extremely rare for British pop records of the time to contain so many self-penned songs, and the group's albums, while including a fair number of American covers, featured an unusual proportion of original tracks. It is difficult to explain to anybody who wasn't around at the time, but the Beatles simply did not *sound* like any British act one had heard before. Their harmonic structures were completely different and, although most of the songs were firmly rooted in a rock-and-roll tradition, their blending of raw rock rhythms with extraordinarily rich and distinctive melodies created music of unprecedented vitality. By the end of 1963 they were, paradoxically, the most raucous *and* the most melodic artists to have emerged into mainstream pop.

If *Please Please Me* was the first truly convincing British rock-and-roll album, *With the Beatles* was perhaps an even greater achievement. Today it seems to signify a genuine turning-point in the development of popular music, the point at which the Beatles fully mastered their early style, combining their beloved rock and roll with tunes bearing their own joyous imprint. The most striking example of this was Paul's 'All My Loving'. A momentous accomplishment, the song combines the excitement of rock-and-roll rhythms with an irresistible melody; it has since been adapted for cover versions which run the gamut of twentieth-century musical styles and genres. By comparison, their excellent cover of Chuck Berry's 'Roll Over Beethoven' is, for all its earnest enthusiasm, the least interesting track on the LP. At any rate, nearly forty years after they were first released those two albums still constitute an utterly explosive assault on the senses.

It was obvious that the Beatles were unlike most British bands of the early sixties in another respect. As well as their obvious musical strengths, their image was irresistible. If there is one word that encapsulates their appeal it is 'authenticity', since the Beatles were so unlike any other mainstream British act that had gone before. They were clearly – although never self-consciously – working class, a far cry from the cosy 'youth club' wholesomeness of Cliff Richard or the rather contrived Cockney chirpiness of Tommy Steele. When the Beatles were interviewed by the press or on television they teased the journalists and broadcasters mercilessly with affable Scouse goodwill; they were simultaneously witty, cutting, rude, sarcastic, charming and cute. Each interview was like a good-natured confrontation, a verbal fencing-match that the Beatles would invariably win. They didn't so much chat to the media as take it on. They were never dull. Unlike many of the 'pretty boy' crooners that preceded them, there was an element of unpredictability and danger whenever they appeared or were interviewed. It was clear that they had intelligence and individuality and, although they openly discussed their relationship with their manager, Brian Epstein, it was obvious that they were not his puppets. They knew they were good, but they weren't arrogant or pretentious, and they always had a good word for other artists. Their appeal was relentless and infectious. Crucially, they had the product to support the swagger.

Shooting for the film that was later to become *A Hard Day's Night* finally began in March 1964. By this point the Beatles were, quite literally, *everywhere*. They didn't so much arrive as explode into the public consciousness. Their appearance at the Royal Command Performance, their unprecedented success in North America, a brace of huge hit singles and the emerging phenomenon of Beatlemania ensured that they were rarely out of the newspapers. Although the shelf life of such a pop phenomenon was still an unknown quantity, the Beatles had quelled worries about their short-term durability in the run-up to shooting. When the film had first been mooted, they were already hugely popular British stars. By the time we came to shoot it, they had become, without a shadow of a doubt, the four most recognizable people on the planet. Their records now had a virtual stranglehold on singles and LP charts throughout the world, and their first record-breaking appearance on the *Ed Sullivan Show* in the USA garnered an audience of around 73 million viewers. A vast wave of Beatles magazines, books, clothing and merchandise swept through the stores of North America and Europe, making them the most visible pop stars since the rise of Elvis. And, although initially perceived as a predominantly teenage phenomenon, enthusiastic high-brow reviews in such establishment organs as *The Times* clearly demonstrated that their popularity went far beyond the predominantly working-class teenage audience that had formed the core of their support in the formative years.

The film was to be directed by a young American expatriate called Richard Lester. Producer Walter Shenson assigned Richard to the project after he had directed a comedy called *The Mouse on the Moon* for him.[1] Because early spring was traditionally a lean time for film freelancers, we were able to assemble a first-class crew, including Ray Simm, a wonderfully reliable and thoughtful art director, and Gil Taylor, a top cameraman. Alun Owen, Welsh-born but with Liverpudlian roots, produced a tremendous 'day in the life' script, and on 2 March the cameras began to roll on the film which American critic Andrew Sarris was later to describe as the '*Citizen Kane* of jukebox movies'.

I met the Beatles for the first time on the set of the movie itself, on the first day of shooting at London's Paddington Station, where we were on board the train to film the opening journey sequences. Having been working so intensively preparing the film's shooting schedule and locations, there had been no previous opportunity to meet up, and prior to this all communications had taken place via Neil Aspinall, then the Beatles' personal assistant and road manager. My first contact with them involved giving them the schedule and explaining in some detail how we were going to shoot the film.

Denise, my oldest child and a teenage 'Beatlemaniac', persuaded me to take her along on that first day so that she could meet her idols. I had reluctantly agreed to this, although I was concerned that it looked somewhat unprofessional. I had no idea what the people behind the lovable image were actually like and how they would respond to their associate producer bringing his daughter along to obtain their autographs. I needn't have worried.

The Beatles were, without question, some of the most charming people I ever met, as was Brian Epstein. While they exhibited the same rapier wit and laconic humour I had seen them demonstrate in television and newspaper interviews, I was genuinely taken aback by their detachment from their extraordinary celebrity. Considering their popularity, they were remarkably well adjusted, which endeared them not only to their fans but to all those who worked with them, making the atmosphere on the set immensely buoyant and good-humoured. Alun did an exceptional job in capturing the essence of their personalities and, while he obviously had to over-simplify certain aspects, the Beatles' on-screen characterizations were fundamentally pretty accurate. Moreover, in front of the cameras they exuded a genuine charm that complemented the script all the way.[2] This was just as well, since the Beatles had never taken acting lessons and had to place themselves entirely in the hands of the film-makers. Remarkably, all of them took to acting extremely easily, Ringo especially. He milked his vulnerable persona perfectly, particularly in his extended solo sequences where he temporarily leaves the group. That said, one of the most effective sustained scenes in the film belonged to George. The sequence in which he deflates a disingenuous London executive (brilliantly played by Kenneth Haigh) was one of the most convincing of the film and was also memorable for introducing the word 'grotty' to an international audience!

The Beatles' infectious sense of bonhomie mitigated the tribulations of the organizational side of filming, which was a nightmare that stretched my negotiating skills to the limit. This was partly due to the Beatles' celebrity and partly to the fact that we were working with a paltry budget of £180,000, a fairly meagre sum even for a pop film. In running the production from one day to the next, I was forced to call in every favour and pull every stunt I could to bring the movie in under budget.

Although Alun's script clearly lent itself to a kind of pseudo-documentary style of shooting, it still required a number of very expensive scenarios, most notably the concert sequence in which the Beatles are seen being filmed for a television show. This we shot at the Scala Theatre in Charlotte Street, London.

As well as the expense of hiring the theatre, there were sequences that required the Beatles to be filmed by onscreen video cameras, and many of Victor Spinetti's scenes took place in a television director's live video-editing control booth. This seems like nothing today, but in 1964 television equipment such as video cameras and playback monitors were astronomically expensive to hire, as technologically they were still in their infancy. On running over the proposed costs, I was appalled to discover that the art department intended to hire the equipment from Bush for £20,000. I realized that the film was in serious danger of running over budget and wracked my brain for a solution. Eventually I came up with a brilliant idea, which, despite being rather devious, could potentially save us a lot of money.

I telephoned Sir Joseph Lockwood, President of EMI, parent company of the Beatles' British label, Parlophone. I got through to his secretary but was informed that Sir Joe was in a board meeting and could not be disturbed. This was no use.

'Could you please tell him that I am the producer of the Beatles' new film and that this is a matter of the utmost urgency.'

Walter was with me at the time and raised an eyebrow as he heard me promote myself to 'producer'. I nodded to him in apology as I waited on the phone. Finally, to my great relief, Sir Joe came on the line. I apologized for getting him out of his meeting and told him – quite falsely – that Bush, one of EMI's main rivals, had agreed to lend us the television equipment we required for filming free of charge in exchange for the publicity it would give them. I said that I was calling to check that this was acceptable to EMI. I must have sounded convincing because his irritated reaction was exactly what I had expected.

'That must not be allowed to happen under any circumstances!' was Sir Joe's response. '*We'll* provide all the equipment that you need without charge.'

'Does that include transport?' I enquired innocently, trying to milk the deal for all it was worth.

'Absolutely,' he said and added that we would have the full co-operation of his company in the transportation, maintenance and operation of all equipment.

I took a deep breath as I put down the receiver. I explained the deal to Walter, who was, from then on, more than happy to let me deputize as the film's producer when the situation demanded. Needless to say, the art department promptly dropped their talks with Bush and Sir Joe was as good as his word, which, I suppose, is more than I could say for myself!

Another stunt that we pulled was to obtain the helicopter seen in the final shot of the film but also used to obtain the aerial shots of the Beatles running wild in a park for the famous 'Can't Buy Me Love' sequence. Under normal circumstances, helicopter hire would have been far too expensive for a film like ours. However, I had an old friend who worked for British European Airways, and I persuaded him to let us use a helicopter stationed at Gatwick. I suggested that we would adapt the 'BEA' logo to spell 'BEATLES' and thus provide them with some cheap product placement! In the end, the deal cost an arrangement fee of a wallet-bursting £25, which made Walter smile as if the heavens had just opened.

Fortunately Richard Lester was a master of spontaneity and responded to the budgetary restraints in a constructive and creative way, frequently turning financial restrictions into stylistic innovations. The 'Can't Buy Me Love' sequence is a great example of this. When we were doing the aerial shots from the helicopter, we realized that there would be a problem with camera shake, but we didn't have the time or the money to obtain gyroscopic stabilization equipment to overcome this. Rather than abandon or postpone shooting, Richard told Gil Taylor to shoot on regardless. In the final edited version the camera shake works beautifully to echo the excitement of the sound-track song and adds a new and experimental dimension to the movie as a whole.

The film is often praised for its innovative and groundbreaking style. The irony is that if we had had stabilization equipment for that sequence we probably would have used it, although it probably would not have ended up half as effective. But clever film-making is about being able to adapt to any given situation, and resourcefulness was always one of Richard's great strengths. His talent for inventing sur-realistic visual jokes was much in evidence throughout the shoot. An example of this can be seen in the 'This Boy' sequence which features a gag where Ringo's 'Walter Raleigh'-style chivalry comes unstuck when the female he is trying to impress falls down a hole in the middle of the road. This wasn't in the script, but Richard saw some workmen digging a hole in the street and improvised. I subsequently paid the labourers a few bob for the use of their hole!

The most serious problems that filming presented were not budget based, however. The most difficult aspect was avoiding the hordes of fans that would appear by lunchtime when they would get wind of the Beatles' whereabouts. By around three or four o'clock in the afternoon, when the local kids were let out of school, things became impossible.

Because we wanted the film to be made in a loose *cinéma-vérité* style, it was vital to incorporate as many real locations as possible, but it was also important to have some kind of production base, some-where we could continue shooting inside when the crowds appeared and made it untenable to film on location. This proved something of a dilemma in the pre-production stage. Studios were prepared only to do block bookings, and we certainly couldn't afford to pay for a sound stage that would remain unused for 70 per cent of the time. Eventually

I hit on the solution of using Twickenham Studios, which had been closed down for some time. I called the owner, Ken Shipman, about the possibility of having them reopened for us at an affordable price, and fortunately he was amenable. It is gratifying that the studios have remained open ever since; for many years after this I enjoyed the pick of the office space there without charge.

Having the use of the studios eliminated a great many of the potential delays and hassles that an all-location film inevitably faces. But each day was a huge game of cat-and-mouse between the film crew and fans, played out on an epic scale across Greater London. The 'prize' for winning was different for both parties. Ours was to bring the film in on schedule and under budget; theirs was to get as close as they could to their idols. It was a game of wit, cunning and intelligence, but it was played out with good nature by both sides, although neither would have wished to admit defeat.

Sometimes our team would win a kind of victory, and we would get through the best part of the day before the fans would find us and come screeching and screaming round the street corners to assault their heroes. Other days it was not so easy. The biggest problem was filming the train scenes. I wanted to shoot these sequences on a genuine moving train, which pleased Richard who was glad to be working closely with someone who shared his vision and who was prepared to go the extra distance to achieve the necessary effect. We both abhorred the idea of shooting the sequences in a studio using back-projected images and refused to settle for the cheapest and most convenient option.

I chartered a train expressly for shooting purposes, a complicated process that took three weeks to negotiate with British Rail, as we had to use one that would constantly change routes in order to evade the fans. I also had to find ways around the technical problems of shooting on the train – not an easy task given the cumbersome sound and camera equipment. We had makeshift camera dollies specially built to fit the walkways and aisles of the train's interior and a carriage fitted out with a power generator. Despite the fact that the train constantly changed its route, information would leak out and kids would be waiting wherever the train pulled up or, worse, throwing themselves on to the tracks! Still, in the end it was worth it, and I think the finished film is far better for the authenticity that the real locations provided. Moreover, the enormous effort that *A Hard Day's Night* took to organize helped cement what was to become an excellent working relationship between Richard and myself.

Sometimes there were more unusual matters to deal with. One day when we were working on the concert footage at London's Scala Theatre my production assistant, Barry Melrose, approached me with some rather bizarre news. Outside in the battle zone, among the hordes of teenage fans gathered round the theatre doors, was an unkempt middle-aged man who said his name was Freddie and who claimed to be John Lennon's long-estranged father. He had been waiting for some hours and insisted on coming into the theatre to see his son. I didn't know anything about John's difficult family history at the time – that he hadn't seen his father since he was a young child – and I knew nothing of the bitterness and resentment John felt towards the parent he thought had deserted him. Still, the situation seemed sensitive, so rather than have the assistant allow him directly on to the set I approached John and told him about Freddie.

'Tell him to fuck off,' said John.

'OK,' I replied and went outside to find his father. I wasn't relishing the idea of relaying this message, but what else was there to do?

'John wants you to fuck off,' I told him.

And that was it. He fucked off!

Actually, that wasn't quite it. John and Freddie did later have some sort of reconciliation, John helping out his father financially over the years, although by all accounts their dealings with one another were never easy.[3]

Their fraught relationship was in marked contrast to that between Paul and his father, Jim, whom he adored. A couple of days after the incident with Freddie, Paul and I were chatting during a break in the

AT THE APPLE'S CORE

shooting of the television concert finale. 'It's me dad's birthday soon,' he said.

'Oh really?'

'Yeah, and I don't know what to buy him.'

Now at that time I bred and raced thoroughbred horses. It so happened that the previous week, while watching some horse-racing, I had been approached by the International Racing Bureau to investigate the possibility of getting the Beatles to attend a race meeting for publicity purposes. I had told them that this was impossible since the Beatles had no interest whatsoever in horses. However, I had met Paul's father on one or two occasions and suspected he liked the odd flutter.

'Does he ever have a bet, Paul, your old man?'

'Yeah, he sometimes used to have a bet, a shilling each way on whatever.'

'Why don't you buy him a racehorse?'

'What?'

'Why don't you buy him a racehorse if he likes to bet?'

He paused for a moment, as the idea took hold. 'How much are they?'

I laughed. 'That depends on the horse. About a thousand pounds might get you something that could win a little race somewhere.'

'It's a great idea. Will you do it? Will you get one for me?'

And I did. The following week I acquired on Paul's behalf a three-year-old bay gelding called Drake's Drum. The problem was hiding the horse until Jim's birthday. We obviously didn't want any news getting out. I called an old friend of mine, Lieutenant Colonel Wilfred Lyde, one of the most respected trainers in the business who was training one of my horses. I said, 'Wilfred, I've got an idea for something, but I can't talk to you about it on the phone.' There was a very real risk that any phone call one made involving the Beatles would get back to the press, and I required complete secrecy.

So the following week I went to see Wilfred, and it was all

36

arranged. He had Drake's Drum collected, taken to his training stables at Spigot Lodge in Yorkshire and hidden there until Jim's birthday. We couldn't start training him because news of Paul's involvement might have leaked out. However, this didn't stop him from asking me if it was possible for him and his girlfriend, actress Jane Asher, to visit Spigot Lodge to see the horse. Because it was impossible for them to stay in a hotel without major hassle I arranged for the couple to stay with the Lydes.

The Lydes, from a different generation and steeped in upper-class formality, knew very little about Paul or the Beatles. They lived in an entirely different world. To their great credit, however, they were only too happy to play hosts to the celebrities. While I was pleased to have arranged the weekend, I would be lying if I said that I wasn't anxious about how the two couples, with their completely different backgrounds of class and age, would get on. After all, Paul, a working-class pop star, and Wilfred, ex-army and some four decades his senior (who still insisted on his weekend dinner guests wearing black tie), seemed somewhat mismatched bedfellows.

Yet, as it turned out, everything was fine when I called the house shortly after Paul's and Jane's arrival.

'How are things going, Wilfred?' I enquired somewhat uneasily.

'Denis, we are having an absolutely splendid time. Things are going very well. What a charming young couple they are!'

I breathed a sigh of relief. On the Sunday Paul phoned me to say that they had had a thoroughly enjoyable time racing with Wilfred. A few weeks later the trainer told me that his one slightly awkward moment at the racetrack had been when Jane had unwittingly followed him into the weighing-in room, at that time a strictly male domain. Wilfred had, with great dignity, drawn himself up to his full height and, taking his mini-skirted companion firmly by the arm, announced, 'This young lady's with me', before steering her out to less hallowed surroundings. I think the Lydes were somewhat perplexed by the younger and more 'with it' staff and servants at Spigot Lodge who bagged the sheets that Paul and Jane had slept in to keep as souvenirs!

To me, the weekend says a great deal about the Beatles' ability to communicate across boundaries of generation and class. In so doing they played an important part in breaking down the 'us' and 'them' class distinctions that had been such a feature of the forties and fifties and that had made Britain seem so staid and stuffy. They were a powerful force in helping to establish the arrival of an increasingly mobile and less class-ridden society.

After the visit to Yorkshire Paul asked me if I could get a portrait of the horse for him. He had realized that it would be impossible to take Jim to Yorkshire to see the horse on his actual birthday because of the group's hectic work schedule, but he figured that a portrait would be an excellent way to introduce his father to his gift. I then contacted a man called Rouch, an extremely conservative character steeped in the hierarchical lore of the sport. To persuade him to make a study of a horse without a fashionable pedigree wasn't an easy task, but eventually he agreed. I gave it to Paul, who was thrilled.

Jim's sixty-second birthday fell on the day after the British première of *A Hard Day's Night*, which took place amid incredible scenes of Beatlemania at the London Pavilion. Afterwards we made our way to the Dorchester Hotel for the party. I was discussing the film with Princess Margaret and her husband Lord Snowden when Paul signalled me over from the other side of the room. I politely excused myself and, leaving them talking to Walter, made my way over to Paul who was with his father. Taking me to one side, the Beatle whispered, 'I've got the picture with me. Let's give it to him now.'

Wishing him a happy birthday, Paul gave the framed and wrapped portrait to Jim, who opened it, examined it and then looked at Paul.

'It's very nice. Thanks.'

'Happy birthday, Dad. Do you like it?'

'Very nice.'

There was a rather empty silence.

I whispered to Paul, 'Did you tell your dad we actually got him the horse?'

'Oh no! Dad, we got you the horse!'

'What do you mean?'

'We got you the horse.'

Jim was incredulous and delighted.

Shortly afterwards I arranged for Jim to visit Spigot's Lodge to see Drake's Drum. Thrilled by the success of his present, Paul called me to ask if we could have the horse entered in a race.

'We can't run him yet. He's not done any serious work,' I told him.

'Let's run him anyway.'

Despite my protests Paul insisted that we enter the horse in a race. Eventually I put it to Wilfred – who was also against the idea – that we could get the horse entered at Chester. He began to protest, but I told him Paul was adamant and the result didn't matter: win, lose or draw. And – can you believe it? – he almost won, taking second place in a race he had no real right even to enter! In the event, Paul was away at the time, but Jim and Paul's brother Michael were there for the first of many a good day's racing, as Drake's Drum went on to win several races during his career.

Many years later, in the early nineties, I was taking care of some business at Twickenham Studios when I happened to bump into Linda McCartney. She and Paul were there for a meeting about Paul's *Get Back* 'comeback' concert film that Richard Lester had directed. We chatted like old friends for a few moments, and I asked after Paul, who was still in the throes of what sounded like some fairly heavy discussions.

'Let me go and get him,' she said.

'Don't worry,' I told her. 'Just give him my best.'

'Are you kidding? He'd never forgive me if he knew you'd been here and hadn't come and said hello.'

Off she went and, sure enough, she reappeared a couple of minutes later with Paul in tow. He seemed very happy to see me and, as we reminisced about the old days, the subject of Drake's Drum came up.

'We've still got that old horse that we gave my dad, you know,' he told me. 'Linda and I still ride him.'

I left Twickenham in good spirits that day. It was rather heart-warming to hear that the horse was still alive and that they still cared for it after all those years. Yet the memory is tinged with a certain sadness. It was the last time I saw Paul and Linda together.

It hardly needs saying that *A Hard Day's Night* was an enormous commercial and critical success that surpassed all expectations, garnering Oscar nominations for Alun's script and George Martin's score. The Beatles' performances were also highly praised, one or two reviewers even comparing them, rather inappropriately, to the Marx Brothers.

It could so easily have been a different story. When the film was first shown to the United Artists executives they were concerned that American audiences wouldn't understand the boys' accents and be able to follow the dialogue. It seems incredible now, but at one stage it was suggested that the Beatles' voices be dubbed by professional actors! Fortunately the idea was vetoed. Can you imagine how dreadful that would have been? It would have totally undermined the authenticity that is the essence of the film's appeal.

The film also spawned a fine LP. If the band's albums can be split roughly into three periods (1963–4, 1965–7 and 1968–70), many would consider *A Hard Day's Night* the best of the first four, the *Beatles for Sale* LP which followed at the end of 1964 appearing less well recorded and less interesting musically by comparison. The soundtrack also turned out to be the only Beatles album with songs composed entirely by John and Paul and included their first really successful self-penned ballads such as 'And I Love Her' and 'If I Fell', as well as John's beautiful 'I'll Be Back' which was not featured in the film. Ballads would become increasingly important to John's and Paul's output and, although the LP contains some traditional rock and roll (John's memorable title track, for example), the love songs enabled the Beatles to showcase their extraordinary harmonic dexterity to the full. The album also provided the first real evidence of their ability to pastiche other styles of music in Paul's wonderful 'And I Love Her', performed in the style of a Latin ballad complete with a deftly executed flamenco guitar solo from George. This ability was to become central to many of their future compositions, including 'Yellow Submarine' (playground singalong), 'When I'm 64' (twenties music hall), 'Your Mother Should Know' (thirties-style Hollywood musical number) and 'Let It Be' (hymn).

The album and the film worked wonders for the Beatles' ever-increasing global popularity and consolidated the success of their recent American visit. Astonishingly, the film is one of the very few examples in movie history that was in profit before it opened, thanks to United Artists' share of the vast advance orders on the soundtrack LP. Moreover, the film's critical reputation has grown continuously in the years since it was made – and rightly so. It is, in retrospect, *the* rock movie *par excellence*, a completely new take on a genre whose insipidness was fast leading to its own demise. It was totally different to all that had gone before, and its imagery and ideas have been hugely influential on subsequent pop movies as well as pop promos and videos. If nothing else, it was the first pop musical to realize that it could be more exciting to combine music with action sequences which were not performance-based. This approach has, of course, since become the aesthetic cornerstone of the pop video and has changed the language of musical presentation for ever.

But *A Hard Day's Night* is more than that. Film-making, perhaps more than any other artistic medium, is a collective creative endeavour. It is extremely rare for a film to work completely, with all of its key elements of screenplay, direction, performances, design, costume and soundtrack gelling seamlessly. Most films have elements that are more successful than others or fail to combine their various components into a satisfying unified whole. But, like *The Third Man* or *Taxi*

Driver, A Hard Day's Night is a genuine exception, a film that blends a wonderful script, inventive direction, a memorable soundtrack and solid performances effortlessly into a singular vision. If the term 'classic' can be applied to a movie, then *A Hard Day's Night* is as deserving of the label as any film I can think of. The Beatles would of course make many more films, most of which I would be involved with. All would be interesting, some exceptionally so. Some might even be called great. But they would never make another perfect film. Even the Beatles weren't that lucky!

2

How the War Was Won

THROUGHOUT MUCH OF July 1965 I was in Madrid working on United Artists' new production, *A Funny Thing Happened on the Way to the Forum* with Zero Mostel and Phil Silvers. As chance would have it, on 2 July the Beatles were to play the Plaza de Toros de Las Ventas, a well-known bullring in town. Many of the younger members of the crew knew of my Beatles connection and, since all official tickets to the concert had long been sold, I agreed to try calling Brian Epstein's management company, NEMS (North End Road Music Stores), to get some complimentary ones. I called their London office to get the name and number of the hotel where the boys were staying and dialled the hotel with the intention of speaking to Neil Aspinall, who I knew would be with the group.

To my surprise John answered. He seemed in good cheer. 'Denis, how are you?'

'Fine.'

'Where are you?'

'I'm here in Madrid.'

'Come over for a cup of tea.'

I explained about the ticket situation.

'Yeah, of course we can sort something out. Just get yourself over here.'

I arrived at the hotel at around half past three and chatted with John and the other Beatles for a while. I was pleased to see them, and I think they were happy to see a familiar face. At around five o'clock they had to leave to get to the bullring to prepare for the evening concert.

'Come with us,' said John.

The next half-hour was a complete blur. I was hustled out of the hotel by the back stairs with the group past hordes of screaming fans who had amassed outside and were filling the streets in the hope of stealing a brief glimpse of their idols. It seemed as though we were walking on a bumpy cushion of air, our feet only intermittently hitting the ground as we were jostled into the waiting limousine. Big Alf Bicknell, the Beatles' chauffeur, stepped on the gas and we were on our way, surrounded by a vast entourage of Guardia Civil and mounted police whose job it was to part the waves of the vast human ocean through which we had to set sail.

But there was only so much any security set-up could do in the wake of the frenzy that Beatlemania inspired. Most countries the Beatles visited were used to providing a safe passage for royals, celebrities and other such dignitaries, but this level of fanaticism over a group of entertainers was unprecedented. There were always too many fans to contain and too much determination on their part to get close to the group, whatever it took. Kids threw themselves in the path of the car, clambered on to the hood and hurled themselves at the windows. Faces would appear momentarily, pressing themselves tightly against the glass until they would fall or be ripped away by security officials or rival fans jockeying for position.

I remember thinking later how incredible, even miraculous, it was that nobody was actually killed in those middle years of the group's career when the mania was at its height. Yet inside the car the Beatles were perfectly composed. They behaved as if they were on a casual Sunday afternoon drive in the country. Of course they had become accustomed to this sort of madness over the past three years and took everything in their stride. Until we reached the bullring, that was!

After more hassle we were prised out of the limo and hustled into the Beatles' dressing-room. That is, if you could call it that. It was actually an infirmary for dying or seriously wounded bullfighters, complete with slabs for the dead and all manner of sinister-looking medical equipment. There were none of the usual home comforts or luxurious touches of artist hospitality one would expect, such as flowers, food, drinks, comfortable chairs and nicely decorated walls. It was just a clinical-white medical room for the gored and the dead. The foreboding atmosphere soon affected the group, who were visibly shaken, and the two-hour wait before the start of the concert seemed to last for ever. They were terrified of going on stage that night. Conversation would come in fits and starts, while the murmurs in the arena gradually built into a crescendo of shouts and screams as the crowd's anticipation grew and the performance became ever more imminent.

It occurred to me that the sinister atmosphere in the infirmary was not the only source of tension. The Beatles were, of course, seasoned professionals by this time and were not given to stagefright in any conventional sense. In fact, the frequency with which they performed together without being able to hear anything the other members of the group sang or played had turned them into the tightest unit of musicians imaginable. What concerned them was their security. The early sixties had already seen a number of tragic and high-profile assassinations, including that of President Kennedy, and, although they could handle most of the situations that fame threw at them, going on stage had become a test of nerves. The Beatles were by then the four most famous people in the Western world, and every time they went on stage they were exposed to tens of thousands of hysterical fans. Security at concert venues was not particularly rigorous in those days, and there was concern that a crazed fanatic could smuggle a firearm into a venue and blow them away on stage.

I wished them luck and went backstage to listen to the performance. Not that anyone could actually hear any music. It was almost totally submerged below the cacophony of thousands of youthful cries and screams, a sound not unlike that of a jet plane taking off at close proximity. But then a Beatles concert had little, if anything, to do with listening to music. Rather, it was as though the young came to pay some sort of tribute or homage to the group by seeing them in the flesh. They were the new secular gods of the young, and simply to see their idols was what counted above all else.

While awe-inspiring, the fervour the concerts generated was not a little terrifying, and I have never forgotten that evening in Madrid. It is not every night you get to enter what John later called the 'eye of the hurricane' and then exit into the hurricane itself. On that occasion I did and, while it was just another day in the life of the Beatles it is an experience I have never forgotten.

Reflecting on the madness of Beatlemania some years later, George said that although the public gave their money the Beatles gave their nervous systems, which is not quite such an easy thing to part with. As they say, 'fame has its price'. Many modern entertainers bemoan that price, the pressures and stresses their fame exerts, the lack of privacy it entails and the concerns over security it engenders. They have every right to feel concerned but would do well to remember that the Beatles paid at least ten times more for their success than any enter-tainers of the past century in the space of just two or three short years. John would, of course, eventually pay the ultimate price.

I couldn't be involved in the second Beatles film, *Help!*, in 1965, as I was busy making another movie, *The Bedford Incident*. However, it did reunite the group with many of those involved in *A Hard Day's Night*, including Richard Lester. *Help!* was, I feel, something of a low for the group, born largely out of the contractual obligation to pro-duce two more films for United Artists as quickly as possible. It does boast some remarkable musical sequences (most notably the 'Ticket to Ride' scene shot in the Austrian Alps), but, for the most part, I feel that *Help!* is a movie whose groundbreaking reputation is disproportion-ate to its qualities. It hasn't aged anything like as well as *A Hard Day's Night*. In fact, in some respects it can be seen as the nadir of the

Beatles' career, and I think it's fair to say that it is probably the weakest of all their pictures.

It would have been pointless to repeat the pseudo-documentary style of their previous film, and I think that Richard was correct to acknowledge this and take a different route. The difficulty was, however, that he was limited by the fact that the Beatles weren't sufficiently adept as actors to carry a full-blown fantasy or action movie at this point, especially when they had become more interested in smoking pot than making films. The film fails to negotiate this problem in an appropriate way, and a fundamental problem is Charles Wood's uncharacteristically weak screenplay. While Alun Owen's script for the previous film resolved the Beatles' limitations as actors by giving them short snippets of dialogue in keeping with their real-life personalities, Wood's script was too demanding and failed fully to appropriate the sharp laconic wit of *A Hard Day's Night*.

Not only that, the music represented little more than a holding operation. With the exception of three wonderfully powerful tracks from John (the title track, 'You've Got to Hide Your Love Away' and 'Ticket to Ride'), the music lacked the excitement of the previous soundtrack. While Paul's solo effort 'Yesterday' – featured on the British soundtrack album but not in the film – requires no further praise or discussion, his contributions to the actual film music were, for all their professionalism, rather more workmanlike. 'The Night Before' was a fairly lacklustre rhythm-and-blues work-out and 'Another Girl' a throwaway country pastiche lacking in genuine inspiration. Despite the predictably massive sales of the LP, it would not be until *Rubber Soul*, released later that year, that the Beatles would produce another album that fully reflected their talents and which restored their exacting standards of quality control.

I think the Beatles realized these problems themselves. They certainly couldn't be bothered to apply themselves seriously to their acting – John later telling me that he was so stoned throughout the shooting that he could remember virtually nothing about it. Although the film does have some wonderfully clever touches, the Beatles' insipid performances, the tiresome plotting and directionless satire ultimately fail to gel into a satisfying whole. Only when the Beatles perform their songs does the film truly ignite, and Richard again exhibits his characteristic gift for extracting the visual essence of a song with great panache. Unfortunately, these sequences are few and far between, and the narrative suffers as a consequence.

Although the picture performed well commercially, John said famously that he felt like an extra in his own movie, a comment which I think is characteristically astute, as the film seems to have nothing of the Beatles' essence in it. Whereas *A Hard Day's Night* managed to condense the frivolity, excitement, charm and personal magnetism of the group into ninety minutes of celluloid, in *Help!* the Beatles are mere passengers in a film that fails to repeat the trick. Looking at it now, it seems like an unfortunate by-product of mid-sixties Beatlemania, the filmic equivalent of the aptly titled *Beatles for Sale* LP: the result of a lapse in quality control brought about by an insatiable desire for new product.

There would be no such problems with quality control for the group's final major release of 1965, the *Rubber Soul* album issued in the UK on 3 December. The album has won many champions over the years and not without good cause. With *Rubber Soul* the Beatles were moving forward yet again into uncharted waters and producing work that was utterly compelling and spellbinding.

Lyrically they were taking giant steps forward, injecting their songs with a poetic sensibility and complexity rarely, if ever, heard on a pop record. On *Rubber Soul* John and Paul took listeners beyond the relative lyrical simplicity of their previous songs. Their music no longer revolved entirely around love songs – that staple of most pop music at the time – and started to become more introverted, reflective and personal. Although with the exception of John's brilliant 'Nowhere Man' and George's memorable 'Think for Yourself' most of the songs are still romantic, the words are much more carefully considered, more self-consciously poetic, more subtle and challenging than before. The boy-meets-girl theme of 'You're Going to Lose That Girl' and 'She Loves You' was replaced by a far greater emotional range from the elusive (John's thinly disguised tale of infidelity, 'Norwegian Wood') to the philosophical (John's and Paul's 'The Word') and from the cynical (Paul's Jane Asher-inspired 'I'm Looking Through You') to the hopelessly romantic (John's 'Girl' and 'In My Life' and Paul's 'Michelle'). Only in the leaden closing number, John's 'Run for Your Life', is the spell broken. He knew this only too well himself and later announced that he hated it.[1]

Musically, too, the Beatles were taking enormous strides, and the album boasted an even richer weave of musical textures than *Help!* or *A Hard Day's Night*. On 'Norwegian Wood' George introduced the Indian sitar to the Beatles' sound, signposting the direction that his own compositions would take for the next two years. In 'The Word' and 'Think for Yourself' Paul's tremendously melodic bass-playing came to the fore, and George Martin contributed a marvellous sustained harpsichord solo to lay the musical icing on John's pretty and reflective 'In My Life'. John's acoustic rhythm guitar shimmered majestically throughout, as did George's chiming solos. Ringo's drumming was as inventive, imaginative and thoughtful as ever. For the Beatles, if not their legions of fans, the days of 'Love Me Do' and 'I Want to Hold Your Hand' now seemed little more than a distant memory.

An altogether more satisfying LP than anything the group had yet released, *Rubber Soul* stands today as a tribute to their desire for expansion and innovation. Incredibly for such an outstanding and appealing record it contained no singles, although the Overlanders saw their chance and took their version of 'Michelle' to the top of the charts. In the mid-sixties it was considered bad form to fill an LP with pre-released material, although the Beatles could easily have issued their own version without too many eyebrows being raised. Instead they chose to release concurrently a double A-side recorded during the same sessions, the joyous 'We Can Work It Out', which was paired with the swaggering 'Day Tripper'. The fact was, the Beatles were so productive at this point in their career that they didn't need to be stingy with their releases. John and Paul were mining a rich vein in their songwriting. They could produce global best-sellers at the drop of a hat.

The Bedford Incident, the film I was producing at the time *Help!* was being shot, starred Richard Widmark and Sidney Poitier and was directed by James B. Harris, who had been Stanley Kubrick's producer on *Dr Strangelove* two years earlier. The film had pacifism as a major theme, which anticipated my next Beatles-related project in a way I could never have foreseen at the time. This was *How I Won the War*, a movie that I produced with Richard Lester in 1966 and which featured John as the bumbling Private Gripweed.

Getting John to do the film was something that Richard and I had privately discussed but which wasn't broached seriously until shortly before filming began. United Artists had agreed to put up around £1 million for the picture, but when we came to work out the prospective budgets we couldn't bring them below £1.25 million. The foreign locations and military equipment required were not going to come cheap. I could understand the studio's reluctance to give us more. A million for a film like this was already a lot of money. But that didn't help us. We needed another quarter of a million, and if we didn't get it the film would not get made.

It was something of a long shot, but I thought it might be worth asking Brian Epstein for some investment. After all, he had a definite soft spot for the film industry, and at the very least I could sound him out about getting John involved. I went to see him at NEMS and explained our financial problems.

Brian was in great spirits when I arrived. 'No problem, Denis. We'll put up the rest of the money.'

This was music to my ears. Since Brian was in such a good mood I thought I'd ask him if he thought John would be interested in the Private Gripweed role.

'Why don't you go and ask him yourself?' he replied. 'He's in the next office.'

I explained to John that the film was essentially an anti-war piece and joked that his character had a wonderful death. John agreed to play the part on the spot, and I came away from NEMS with John Lennon on board and an extra quarter of a million, which wasn't bad for an afternoon's work! As it turned out, we didn't need Brian's money, as I managed to make some crucial savings later in the production stage, but I'll never forget the generosity and loyalty of his gesture. Of course he would have stood to gain had the film done well at the box office, but I think he genuinely wanted to help us make the movie happen.

The first major shooting for *How I Won the War* took place in Celle, West Germany. I feel John agreed to be involved in the picture for a number of reasons. Although he had no particular aspirations to become an actor, he had an excellent working relationship with Richard and me and a strong sympathy with the film's theme. Crucially, he was available just then to work on the project, as the Beatles had recently completed what was to be their final series of concerts. So while Paul remained in London composing the score to the Boulting Brothers' film *The Family Way* and George jetted off to India to study the sitar, John flew over to join us in West Germany and Spain to work on the picture.

It was obvious that for his character to be remotely credible he would have to have a military-style haircut. This caused him some trepidation, as he did not like the idea that the press or other hangers-on would wait around and collect the hair clippings to sell them off to fans. I said, 'Don't worry. We'll do the cut in a hotel room, and you can dispose of the clippings afterwards yourself.'

And so John had his haircut. The press were kept out, as were most of the crew, although Brian Epstein and Neil Aspinall were present. My son, Shaun, then aged fifteen, who was helping out in the camera department during his school holidays, was also with us. Spotting an opportunity to bag a unique piece of Beatles memorabilia, he asked John if he could take some of the hair.

John nodded and told him, 'Now you're the only one with a piece of my hair!'

Shaun thought about it. 'But nobody will ever believe that it's yours.'

John smiled. 'Well, it isn't.'

We were all mystified by this bizarre statement. We had just seen the hair being cut off John. A bemused silence descended upon the room, as we waited for enlightenment.

'Give me something to write with,' John demanded, with comic impatience.

Shaun handed him a hotel postcard and a pen, and the Beatle began scribbling on the card, as Brian, Neil, Shaun and myself looked on transfixed. A moment later, he handed the card back to Shaun, who smiled before showing it to the rest of us. It read: 'This is to certify that this *was* my hair. John Lennon.'

The Beatles' fame was such that the next day John's haircut made international headlines. The press reported that the clippings had been burned. And so they were. But Shaun, now a successful cameraman, still has the lock of hair and the certificate given to him all those years ago by a generous if somewhat world-weary star.

John went through intermittent stages of being simultaneously bored and anxious as the film rolled into action. He was never very happy on the set. He felt like a fish out of water. In *A Hard Day's Night* and *Help!* he had had the other members of the band with him, and now he missed both their company and the mutual support that pervaded the atmosphere of the previous films. One day, very early on in the shoot, he came to me looking very worried.

'I don't know what I'm doing with all this, Denis,' he confided.

'What do you mean?'

'All this acting stuff. Having to work with all these real actors. I feel like I'm out of control.'

I suggested that he talk things over with Richard, who I hoped, as director, would be able to reassure him with regard to any concerns he had over his acting or any other aspect of filming.

I didn't know at the time what Richard said to John – or even for sure that he had taken my advice – but he never looked quite so uneasy again. I am sure that this was partly because we made every effort to keep him occupied from then on. While we were in Almeria, southern Spain, where the bulk of the shooting took place, I encouraged John's friends to come to stay with him in the huge mansion he and Cynthia were sharing with Michael Crawford, the film's other main star, and his wife Gabrielle. The house had been the estate of a family for many years, and the last in line, an old woman in her nineties, had only recently died, so there was much talk of ghosts. Brian, Ringo and Neil all came out to visit at various times, and John would occupy himself between takes with his acoustic guitar, picking out old favourites for the crew and, more famously, composing the song that would eventually come to be regarded as one of his greatest works. I don't think that it was a coincidence that 'Strawberry Fields Forever' was written in Spain; it evokes a longing for home that was to grow more intense as the movie progressed.

John couldn't have been more relieved when the final day of shooting came to an end. He wanted out as soon as possible and was itching to get on the next plane to London. Normally it is not quite that simple at the end of a shoot. Before stars can be released and sets can be struck the final dailies have to be sent for processing and viewed by the producer and director to ensure that everything is OK. If one scene or more needs to be reshot later on, the potential costs are enormous, and any delays caused by absent stars can make for further, sometimes crippling financial and logistical complications, so stars are usually not let go before these are checked. I was very reluctant to break with protocol, but John was so anxious to go home that he begged me to let him go straight away.

When he wanted something badly, John was probably the most

persuasive and manipulative person one could come across, battering down any resistance with an irresistible combination of reason and charm. I was very reluctant to let him go, but in the end I agreed, on condition that if anything was wrong with the dailies he would be on the first plane back to Almeria. He was thrilled, and as he was leaving he handed me a copy of his recently published *Penguin John Lennon*. Inside the inscription read: 'To Denis (and Donna), For smiling and sending me home. Thank you! Love, John Lennon.' Fortunately the prints were fine and I didn't have to get him back. It would have been a difficult call, to say the least.

With its pacifist sentiments, *How I Won the War* did not achieve much success at the box office, but it is a film I feel quite proud of. Years later John and I were chatting about the film, and I remembered the conversation we had had on the very first day of shooting. I reminded him of it, and he told me that he had taken my advice and gone to talk to Richard. 'But I realized', he told me, 'that I was in control and Richard was out of control.'

3
Long Hot Summer

NINETEEN SIXTY-SEVEN was to be the Beatles' most eventful and strangest year, full of intense highs and miserable troughs. By the end of this year of flower power and psychedelia they had released their most celebrated single, 'Penny Lane'/'Strawberry Fields Forever', and album, *Sergeant Pepper's Lonely Heart's Club Band*. They had also lost their close friend and business associate, Brian Epstein, laid the foundations for their new company, Apple, and made their first and only critical disaster, *Magical Mystery Tour*, which I helped them produce throughout the summer and autumn of that year.

That first astonishing double A-side single, comprising John's 'Strawberry Fields Forever' and Paul's 'Penny Lane', issued in February 1967, has, without doubt, established itself as one of the greatest record releases of all time. Ironically, it was the first single of the Beatles since 1963's 'Please Please Me' to fail to reach the *Record Retailer* number one slot in Britain, kept off the top of the charts by 'Release Me' by Englebert Humperdinck. Had it reached number one it would have been the Beatles' twelfth successive chart-topper. They were rightly proud of the record, so I'm not sure that the boys were too disappointed, Ringo later commenting that its relative failure came as something of a relief, as it seemed to unburden them from the pressures of public and media expectations. The release of the single, their first of the year, also heralded a change of image for the group.

Although they had by then become more casual in their dress, their universally recognizable appearance in neat tailored suits, with the famous 'Beatle fringe', much evident in *A Hard Day's Night* and *Help!*, had disappeared completely to be replaced by a psychedelic look that embraced drooping moustaches, granny glasses, pickwick jackets and brightly coloured silks.[1] With the arrival of flower power the Beatles morphed into the international figureheads of counterculture, embracing all of its myriad trappings, including meditation, Eastern mysticism, hippy paraphernalia and hallucinogenic drug culture. No longer wishing to be perceived as lovable moptops, the Beatles threw themselves into their new image with great gusto, giving exclusive interviews to the underground press[2] and signing and helping to finance a 'legalize cannabis' petition placed in *The Times*.

The two new songs on the single, originally intended for inclusion on the LP that was to become *Sergeant Pepper's Lonely Hearts Club Band*, were famously based on childhood recollections of fondly remembered Liverpool locations. However, unlike the relatively straightforward sentiment of *Rubber Soul*'s 'In My Life', the nostalgia of the new tracks had a distinctly surreal and hallucinogenic quality, as if the composers were reflecting their recollections through psychedelic rather than rose-tinted spectacles. Despite their similar subject matter, the songs demonstrated the very distinctive styles of their respective authors, John and Paul now working increasingly independently on their compositions. 'Penny Lane' is a typical 'Paul' song, melodic, irresistibly pretty and charmingly sentimental. John's 'Strawberry Fields Forever' is less melodic, more self-consciously poetic, gutsy and lyrically playful, its surrealism bordering in places on full-blown abstraction.

It is dangerous to generalize too much about the individual musical and lyrical 'signatures' of Lennon and McCartney. However, I think that it is fair to say that the 'Penny Lane'/'Strawberry Fields Forever' single is the best example of their respective individual styles preserved on one disc. Moreover, as with all Beatles compositions of this period, each song is beautifully executed with excellent backing from George and Ringo and with the predictably flawless production of George

Martin. Indeed, by this point in their career George had unquestionably become central to the Beatles' ambitious recording processes. The most affable and approachable of individuals, he was also, without doubt, Britain's most gifted record producer. A classically trained musician, his understanding of musical form and technical mastery of instrumentation provided the perfect foil for the untrained musicality of the Beatles, who refused to learn to read music, believing that this would somehow rob them of their intuitive harmonic abilities. Like all great producers, George had a remarkable knack of helping his artists realize their musical visions, and nowhere was this more obvious than on the 'Strawberry Fields Forever'/'Penny Lane' single. It was, after all, George's technical wizardry that joined the two best takes of John's song together, despite the fact that they were in different tempos! And it was George who helped realize Paul's musical vision for 'Penny Lane', obtaining the piccolo trumpet that Paul had fallen in love with while watching a classical concert on the television.

On 1 June 1967 the Beatles released the album whose name has since become almost as famous as the group's own. It is also the record on which a large part of their cultural legacy is staked. The critical reputation of *Sergeant Pepper's Lonely Hearts Club* has unquestionably dwindled somewhat over the last ten years, *Revolver* being regarded increasingly as the Beatles' greatest work. Nevertheless, while that LP certainly contains some fine songs, its critical reputation may not, ultimately, eclipse that of *Sergeant Pepper*. A great piece of work though *Revolver* was, it didn't at the time inspire anything like the commercial success or make the impact of the 1967 album, which managed to tap into the popular imagination in a way that no other individual recording has before or since. According to the critic Langdon Winner, the LP created such a sense of shared international spirit that 'for a brief while the irreparably fragmented consciousness of the West was unified, at least in the minds of the young'. This is obviously something of an exaggeration, but it is difficult to overestimate the cultural impact of that recording. It crystallized and somehow distilled the essence of its age into forty minutes of vinyl – but was also, in some ways, ahead of its time.

Its importance in the development of sound-recording techniques, track sequencing and marketing were also unprecedented. It is all too easy to forget just how many precedents *Sergeant Pepper* set. Even the packaging was revolutionary. As well as sporting what was then the most ambitious and expensive photograph ever to grace an album sleeve, the cover was one of the first in a gatefold format, it was the first pop album to feature printed song lyrics, the first to include novelty giveaway items (pop art cut-outs) and the first to employ a major artist – Peter Blake – for its design. In terms of its songs it may or may not be the Beatles' greatest LP, but in terms of its impact it is certainly the most important. It became the touchstone by which all other records were judged by musicians, songwriters, producers and designers the world over.

I suspect that there are several reasons for its relative unfashionability these days among fans and critics. First, people listen to music differently now. The increasing affordability of records and the advent of remote control, multi-disc facilities, home taping, computer downloading of music and random CD track selection have encouraged shorter attention spans. The days when audiences listened to LPs in their entirety have all but gone. Although not strictly a concept album, *Sergeant Pepper* is the Beatles' *gesamtkunstwerk*, made to be listened to in the order in which the tracks appear on the LP in a single hearing, the songs seguing into each other to create a unity unprecedented in their previous work. To remove a song such as 'Lovely Rita' or 'Good Morning, Good Morning' from its original context reduces its impact hugely. I have often wondered what more serious songwriters and musicians think about having their work cut and pasted into the compilation albums which now seem to occupy such a huge proportion of the record market. I suppose most regard them as a necessary evil.

Secondly, there has been a natural and understandable backlash against the critical wisdom that for years lionized *Sergeant Pepper* to such an extent that the other LPs had a tendency to become somewhat overlooked. This backlash has been exacerbated by the younger generations of critics who did not live through the original *Sergeant Pepper* experience and feel the need to justify themselves by rediscovering, reassessing and re-evaluating the musical heritage of our recent past. *Revolver* is the perfect Beatles album for today's critics, full of marvellous songs and guitar-playing and musically and lyrically pointing the way to the Beatles' next phase. Not only that, with one or two notable exceptions (such as 'A Day in the Life') *Sergeant Pepper* is much more 'Paul's' LP than 'John's', and, since his untimely death, John has inevitably received the most critical attention.

While *Sergeant Pepper* was simultaneously revolutionizing the music industry and occupying the number one position in album charts throughout the world, the Beatles went off to Bangor in North Wales to study transcendental meditation under the Maharishi Mahesh Yogi. It was here, on Sunday 27 August, that they received the news of Brian Epstein's death.

This had an enormous impact on all of us who were connected with the Beatles. While it is true that he was less influential in terms of the band's career after they stopped touring, his tragic death left the group broken-hearted and bewildered. Worse still, the strange circumstances of his death from a drugs overdose created an enormous tide of media speculation as to whether he had committed suicide, despite the coroner's verdict that his death had been accidental. The exact circumstances of his end are destined to remain for ever unknown. A few people have come up with the ridiculous theory that he was the victim of a murder plot, but I think it is certainly possible that he killed himself. Towards the end of his life he was becoming depressed, and he was increasingly reclusive and uninterested in his job as manager.

Brian's death distressed not only the Beatles. He was well liked by many of his business associates, and his passing genuinely saddened me. We had always got along very well, our friendship partly enhanced by a mutual interest in the art of bullfighting. A couple of weeks before his death he was laid up in bed and called me to ask if he could borrow a weighty antiquarian book on the history of the sport I had acquired in Spain and which I had mentioned to him one day over lunch. I had the volume, *La Fiesta Nacional*, sent round to his London residence, joking that he had better not attempt to read it in bed as it might collapse under the weight. It was the last time I spoke to him and, as it turned out, it was the last book Brian would read. It was later recovered from the death scene and returned to me by his assistant, Peter Brown, who found it next to his bed. It now sits on the bookshelf in my study, and I can't help thinking of Brian whenever I look at it.

A great deal has been written about his life, mostly by people who never knew him. His career is forever being reassessed, with much of the attention being given to revisionist considerations of his management of the Beatles. Most of this is negative, focusing on the poor deals he got for the group, usually citing his failure to capitalize on the American merchandising craze of 1964 or his naïvety in some of the Beatles' film negotiations – and it is true that he was naïve or poorly advised when it came to negotiating some of the Beatles' film deals. When negotiating the group's royalty percentage for *A Hard Day's Night*, for example, he pre-empted the United Artists executives' standard offer of 25 per cent by telling them that he 'wouldn't accept less' than seven and a half! Fortunately, Brian's lawyer, David Jacobs, was later able to improve the deal.

It is also true that hundreds of thousands of dollars were lost because Brian initially accepted just 10 per cent of the Beatles' US merchandising rights. Not wanting NEMS to become swamped with enquiries from manufacturers wishing to produce Beatles-related merchandise, Brian appointed an opportunistic young businessman called Nicky Byrne to take over the task. Byrne's companies, Stramsact and Seltaeb, managed to negotiate a whopping 90 per cent of the profits, Brian accepting a derisory 10 per cent for himself and the Beatles. It should, of course, have been the other way around, and millions of pounds were lost before a lengthy legal battle commenced. By the time the situation was improved, the ferocious desire in America for Flip-Your-Wig board games, Ringo Roll cake, Beatle Bar ice lollies and other items of souvenir tat had waned. The moment had gone.

However, it's easy to be critical retrospectively about these deals and wise after the event, and much of the posthumous criticism of Brian's merchandising mistakes is pretty stupid. At the time when he and his advisers made these deals, pop merchandising was in its infancy and, with the possible exception of Elvis, the Beatles' popularity was unprecedented. Nobody knew the full potential or implications of such deals. Sailing in uncharted waters, Brian had nothing to measure his decisions against. Is it fair to criticize him in the light of this? I doubt whether those who are so quick to condemn his deals would have been any the wiser at the time. Anyway, whatever mistakes he may have made are surely disproportionate to his enormous achievements, which these days are in danger of becoming overlooked. Lest these achievements be forgotten, it may be worth reflecting on them for a moment. First and foremost, Brian discovered the Beatles. (That's not quite true actually; the Beatles had been 'discovered' several times before Brian took them on but he was the first person who 'mattered' to discover them.) Crucially, he *understood* them. He repackaged and restyled them, taking difficult decisions when the situation demanded.[3] He presented them to an industry that was very sceptical about the commercial possibilities of provincial pop groups and, when the going got tough, his unshakeable belief in the Beatles proved paramount to their eventual acceptance by George Martin at Parlophone. Make no mistake, without Brian's faith and entrepreneurial drive . . . well, the rest is history.

If this had been his only achievement, we would have a great deal to thank him for. But this wasn't all. In his more generous moments Paul has made some very astute observations about Brian's importance as a cultural locus for the group. Brian's cultured, middle-class upbringing fostered a love of fine art, classical music and theatre. These sensibilities rubbed off on the Beatles, making them interested

61

in art forms other than contemporary popular music and bringing a multi-dimensional quality to their compositions quite distinct from other groups of the time. The relationship between a manager and his artists is a complex one, but I think it is reasonable to suggest that Brian was very important in this way.

Equally important, he had enormous faith in their ability to evolve and change, a fact lost on most of today's commentators. With a few hits under their belt, most managers would have attempted to constrain their artists' desire to stretch themselves musically and to experiment with their image, merely encouraging them to repeat the same old formula until the well ran dry.[4] Brian was possibly the first modern manager to understand that this was not the way to promote longevity and had an instinctive trust of the Beatles' own understanding of pop culture. Dare I suggest that what he *didn't* do may have been as significant as what he did do as a manager? You can put a price on what Brian Epstein 'lost' for the Beatles. You can't put a price on what he gave them.

Shortly after Brian's death I was having lunch with Richard Lester, who was working on a commercial at Isleworth Studios, London, when I received a telephone call that was to have an enormous impact on my life for the next three years. It was John and Paul.

'Denis, it's us! Can you come and meet us in the next few days?'

'Sure. What about?'

'We've been thinking. We want you to come and run us.'

I was elated and enormously flattered that they should turn to me for help.

Two days later I went along to NEMS and met up with John, Paul, Neil and, if memory serves, Peter Brown. It turned out that the Beatles were in the process of forming a new organization – Apple – and that they wanted me to be one of its directors. The group's decision to lay the foundations of this ambitious project was twofold.

The first was purely financial. The Beatles, like all top earners in sixties Britain, were extremely highly taxed. Despite a tolerance of

Harold Wilson's Labour government – in 1964 Wilson, while still leader of the opposition, publicly presented the group with a Variety Club award – they were all too aware that it took a large proportion of their earnings. Before Apple there had been several attempts to reduce their tax burden. The Bahamas locations for *Help!*, for example, had been chosen intentionally so that their earnings from the film could be salted away in an offshore account, although this ruse was later abandoned when Brian decided that tax evasion would be bad for the Fab Four's image. This frustration over their earnings would subsequently inspire George to pen the most damning piece of social criticism the Beatles were to ever to commit to record, the jaundiced, scathing 'Taxman' that opened side one of *Revolver*.

They had been informed by their financial advisers that they had a problem and that they could evade the very high rates of capital gains tax by buying into their own fortune. This would help ensure their financial stability. The establishment of Apple involved the Beatles collatoralizing themselves by buying and incorporating a stake in their own worth for the same price at which their existing company, the Beatles Ltd, was valued. This meant no capital gains and thus no capital gains tax.

The second reason for the creation of Apple was at once personal and philanthropic. In the wake of Brian's death, the Beatles felt they should take a greater part in managing their own affairs and artistic output. They envisaged that founding their own company with a number of different departments would allow them to do just that. Apple was conceived grandly but evolved gradually, on the principle that it would be a multi-faceted master company with a number of divisions encompassing records, films, clothes retail, books and other sectors. It also meant that they could diversify into other areas via a company that could manage and finance aspiring artists from a range of formal disciplines, including musicians, film-makers, designers and writers. The Beatles had great sympathy for young artists who they felt were frequently exploited by the captains of the entertainment industry, or 'men in suits' as John and Paul called them. Part of their plan was based on an idealistic and optimistic assumption that they could make a genuine difference. The Beatles were to be the four main directors, Neil Aspinall would become the managing director, and I was to be made a director of Apple Corps as well as the film and publicity divisions. Although Apple Corps was not formally established until January 1968, the first Apple company had been registered in May 1967, and the first major project credited to the company was the television film *Magical Mystery Tour*, which I was to produce.

The meeting finished late. I left the NEMS offices that evening walking on air. After all, it's not every day you get asked to play a major part in the future of the world's biggest stars. On leaving the meeting I didn't know where to go. Bursting with happiness and pride, all I knew was that I had to find someone to tell who would appreciate the situation. Impulsively I decided to call on my old friend Nic Roeg, whom I had known as a focus puller and later as a cinematographer on films such as *A Funny Thing Happened on the Way to the Forum* and *Petulia*. I arrived at his home in Marylebone, without warning, to discover that he was already tucked up in bed with his actress wife Susan Stevens. I apologized for the intrusion and, sitting on the end of the bed, relayed my news to them over a glass or two of red wine. His career also was progressing well, and he was on the verge of negotiating his directorial début. (The resulting film, *Performance*, a surreal gangster thriller that would star James Fox and Mick Jagger, would seal his reputation as one of Britain's most prominent and controversial talents.) That night, we were full of joy and optimism for the future. I returned home somewhat worse for wear. It had been a great day, perhaps the most exhilarating of my life.

4

The Mystery Trip

PAUL HAD LONG nurtured a desire for the Beatles to direct themselves in their own film. Brian had been well aware of this, although I'm not sure that he had approved. By this point in their career his opinion may not have mattered much to the group anyway.

The first ideas for the *Magical Mystery Tour* film were relayed to me during a meeting at NEMS in early September 1967. Paul's concept, based on a psychedelic bus trip around the English countryside, was possibly inspired by the antics of American writer Ken Kesey's 'Merry Pranksters', a group of stoned hippies who toured the USA in a multi-coloured bus. Their outrageous antics, a seminal happening in sixties psychedelic drug culture, were documented by Tom Wolfe in the *World's Tribune Journal* in early 1967. His account was later expanded and published in book form as *The Electric Kool-Aid Acid Test*. I don't know whether Paul had read Wolfe, although Kesey was later to become involved with Apple's publishing and spoken word recordings projects.[1]

Paul illustrated his idea to me at the meeting by drawing a circle that he split into four segments. Each member of the group would have a section that they would individually write and direct. Nobody knew what exactly, but this could be sorted out in due course. I thought that in principle the concept was a good one. Although no actual scenes were planned at this stage, it seemed to me that Paul's idea had genuine potential. I liked the notion of each member of the group individually creating something of his own and saw the film as a kind of surrealistic portmanteau. I suggested that if we could get four twenty-minute sequences written and directed by each of them I could shoot a further fifteen minutes of linking footage. This, combined with a title sequence, would amount to just under a hundred minutes, enough for a feature film that could possibly obtain a theatrical release.

It never happened. The four were keen to get on and make the film and didn't want to spend time working out the minutiae of script and screenplay. This need not have been a major problem, given the surrealistic and psychedelic nature of the concept. What was going to be much harder to sort out fast were the organizational and logistical difficulties. Having spent many years in the film industry, I knew the importance of pre-production and that starting to shoot a film prematurely would lead to all kinds of nightmares. It seemed impossible to get a productive working arrangement, and I quietly resigned myself to the notion that I would do my best for them on their terms.

Unfortunately my concerns proved well founded. Without adequate preparation the filming inevitably took off in complete chaos. There were all sorts of logistical problems, the Beatles having no idea about the degree of planning necessary to make a successful film. Although they had starred in movies, they knew nothing about their organization and seemed to think that everything would fall into place as they went along. When Brian had been alive it always had. But Brian was dead, and it didn't.

Getting involved in producing and directing their own film was a brave step for a pop group. Like so many of the Beatles' ideas, it was unprecedented at the time. Unfortunately, their attitude was to learn as they went along rather than to find out about the job before taking it on. If they had done so they would probably never have made it! They had absolutely no idea that studios have to be booked weeks or even months in advance, that contracts and union terms have to be negotiated with cast and crew, that locations have to be prepared and all manner of other things arranged. Their decision to curtail the pre-production phase betrayed an inability to comprehend that all filmed entertainments need discussion and careful planning to make them work. While I'm all for improvisation and spontaneity, it's simply not a good idea just to get a few people together, book a few vehicles and some camera equipment and go off without any real idea of who is responsible for what. Not, that is, unless you are prepared to accept that the finished result will look amateurish and ill-thought-out. Great films don't just make themselves.

The Beatles had supreme self-confidence that they could master any medium. In most respects their previous forays into new areas of creativity had been justified and legitimized by some astonishing successes. They had, after all, become increasingly active in their own record production, and I can only guess that this, combined with their success in other areas (Paul with his film score work on *The Family Way* and John with his two best-selling books), had instilled in them the confidence to take on the film industry. Unfortunately film production requires financial and logistical problem-solving skills, commodities the Beatles sorely lacked. And their shortcomings in this department would eventually be their undoing.

Undaunted by my warnings that the film required planning, the Beatles set off from London on their psychedelic bus tour on 11 September 1967, with a bizarre collection of actors, weird and wonderful performers, fan-club members and technicians on board. Over the next week they stopped off at various locations in Hampshire, Devon, Somerset and Cornwall to shoot many hours of mainly improvised footage. I didn't go myself, as it was necessary for me to be based in the production offices. I employed Gavrik Losey, son of the director Joseph Losey, as a production assistant. He was my eyes and ears for the first week of shooting, and we tried to keep in constant touch. There was always going to be a vast number of organizational problems in a shoot that was so loosely structured. How, for example, could accommodation arrangements be made for a group of forty or fifty people who hadn't got a clue where they were likely to end up each evening?

There were other problems. At one point the bus became trapped on a narrow bridge while heading towards Widecombe, Dartmoor, causing massive tailbacks. The huge convoy of journalists which was following the bus didn't help matters either.

I was frequently forced to improvise second-rate solutions at the last minute. An example of this was when I had to book an old disused air hangar at West Malling for the 'Your Mother Should Know' and 'I Am the Walrus' sequences because it was impossible to obtain any studio time at Twickenham, Pinewood or Elstree. We also shot the marathon sequence there. I had just taken delivery of a bright-yellow Iso Revolta sports car and, seeing it driven swiftly around on the runway, inspired the group to improvise a race sequence. I was there to supervise the shooting and ended up, at John's request, appearing in the film as the race starter, firing a pistol to get the mystery tour race under way.

Despite the haphazard shooting, the finished film did contain some remarkable sequences and has since come to be regarded as something of a cult classic. In a sense, it can be seen as the Beatles' cinematic countercultural manifesto, a surreal indictment of the British establishment which, with its cheating vicars, psychotic army drill sergeant and dancing policemen, gently ridicules the pillars of the status quo. And, despite a few rather amateurish sections, the film does contain genuinely brilliant musical sequences, John's 'I Am the Walrus' being an obvious one. My own personal favourite was the wonderful 'Flying' sequence, which we assembled from hours of tinted library footage shot and later rejected by Stanley Kubrick for *Dr Strangelove*. Incredibly, after *Magical Mystery Tour* was first broadcast, I was telephoned by the great director himself. Always intensely protective of his work, he had recognized the footage from five years earlier and demanded to know where we had obtained it. Luckily I had the papers to prove that it had been legitimately acquired, so the situation didn't turn nasty.

Another highlight was Victor Spinetti's wonderful army recruitment scene, where he is seen aggressively barking orders at the bus party until Ringo meekly asks him 'Why?' A veteran of both of the Beatles' previous movies, Victor had been asked to accompany them on the whole of the bus trip but had to decline because he was otherwise engaged. He had been the original choice for the courier role and John, a close friend of Victor's, was disappointed that he couldn't take a bigger role in the film. Nevertheless the pair would team up again the following year to work on the theatrical adaptation of John's classic nonsense verses and stories, *In His Own Write* and *A Spaniard in the Works*. Along with 'rubber man' Nat Jackley and the droll surrealist poet and musician Ivor Cutler, Victor was one of the few actors specifically chosen by the four for inclusion in the film. The rest were picked semi-randomly from the actor's directory *Spotlight* mainly for their appearance rather than their acting experience or ability.

Looking back on the film with the benefit of over thirty years' hindsight, it is apparent that it was, in some respects at least, ahead of its time. Its surreal humour certainly predated Monty Python, and its radical style unquestionably influenced modern pop videos and pop musicals such as the Monkees' *Head* and Frank Zappa's *200 Motels*.

Editing the picture proved pretty difficult. I knew that the Beatles, especially Paul, would want to be involved in the process but realized that it was crucial to obtain the services of a professional editor. After careful consideration I brought in Roy Benson, a long-standing friend of mine and a promising young technician who was later to work on one or two other Beatles-related projects. Unfortunately, there was so much uncatalogued footage and so many disagreements between the group over what to include and what to reject that the editing, which should have taken two weeks, ended up lasting almost two months!

During the film's post-production stage I spent much of my time in distribution negotiations with the American television channels ABC and NBC. Both were dying to get their hands on the film and began a bidding frenzy for US transmission rights. Huge sums were mentioned, the prospect of a brand-new Beatles film all but guaranteeing enormous ratings. To my astonishment, however, Paul wanted the film to be premièred by the BBC, an idea to which I was opposed. Paul insisted, arguing that the corporation had always been good to the Beatles in the past. You can imagine my horror when BBC1 screened the film on Boxing Day 1967 at 8.35 p.m. in black and white. The timing of the transmission could not have been more insensitive. Its screening, at a time traditionally reserved for more conventional forms of family entertainment, was totally inappropriate for an avant-garde film which would have been much more at home in a 10 p.m. slot on BBC2. Worse still, the unfathomable decision to show the movie in monochrome totally undermined its swirling hallucinatory imagery, rendering its aesthetic *raison d'être* completely redundant. To this day, I'm not sure how these decisions came to be made, but it has to be said that they were monumentally stupid.

Adding to the growing list of concerns was the release of the ground-breaking double EP set, a lavish and unprecedented affair complete with gatefold sleeve, cartoon booklet and printed song lyrics. It was supposed to have been put out a couple of weeks before the film was transmitted, allowing the songs to catch with public and critics and to cash in on the Christmas market. Unfortunately there were manufacturing delays, and when it was finally released record dealers didn't know where to place this oddity in their shops. The delayed release (combined with the BBC banning 'I Am the Walrus' from the radio airwaves for the 'offensive' reference to knickers) meant that people had very little time to become familiar with the songs and, like the BBC's bizarre transmission slot, did the film's critical reception no favours at all. To make matters worse, fans were puzzled by the fact that the wonderfully executed strip cartoons of the story by *Beatles Monthly* cartoonist Bob Gibson barely reflected the film's content. This was because of delays in the editing process, in which some of the scenes originally filmed did not make the final cut.

The reviews were disastrous, the next day's newspapers savaging the movie as if it was the most offensive programme ever broadcast.

Rereading some of those reviews today, I feel they say more about their reviewers' lack of cine-literacy than about the film's weaknesses. It seems that most television critics failed to appreciate that the film was intentionally surreal, complaining repeatedly that it had no story. This seems tantamount to complaining that a Kandinsky painting isn't figurative enough.

That said, one can to some extent understand the panning of *Magical Mystery Tour*. After all, the critics were not used to seeing the Beatles appearing like this. Although *A Hard Day's Night* and *Help!* had included some surrealist elements, they both had a basic narrative logic; moreover they had presented an image of the Beatles that critics were familiar and comfortable with. Viewers were aggrieved when what they got instead was a stoned-looking collection of hippies who seemed to have no intention of reprising their boy-next-door, moptop image and, indeed, seemed hell-bent on destroying it for ever. Of course, the image change heralded by 'Strawberry Fields' and *Sergeant Pepper* had pre-empted this, as had their appearance on the first global television transmission *Our World*, in which the group appeared in flower-power regalia and performed 'All You Need Is Love'. There had also been a series of potentially damaging confessions in the media by Paul who, to the horror of the British establishment, openly admitted to having taken LSD. But *Magical Mystery Tour* was much more difficult for the press to swallow, a full-length film conveying the Fab Four's new direction more graphically than an image on an LP cover, a television interview or news report could ever do.

The critical thumbs-down upset the Beatles, who were not used to bad reviews. Until that year it seemed that the group were so universally cherished that they were almost beyond condemnation, that they could do nothing wrong in the eyes of critics and pop fans. Paul, the original instigator of the film, was particularly hurt by the reviews. He spoke to the press in an attempt to defend the project, explaining that it had been intentionally surreal and maintaining that it should be regarded like 'an abstract painting'.[2]

The film was broadcast again a few days later, on 5 January, this time in colour on BBC2, but there was still little enthusiasm for it. The double EP record set that accompanied the film sold very respectably in the UK, and in the USA the songs later comprised the first side of a conventional long-playing album also entitled *Magical Mystery Tour* which was filled out by a brace of recent hits and B-sides. These comprised the 'Penny Lane'/'Strawberry Fields Forever' single, 'Hello, Goodbye', 'Baby You're a Rich Man' and 'All You Need Is Love', their anthemic homage to the summer of love. But that appalling critical mauling, which made front-page headlines in many of the British tabloids, scared off the wealthy American networks, and the film was not shown on US television until several years later. This was a great shame as it meant that the film wasn't transmitted to its largest single audience.

However, as it turned out, all was not lost. Neil and I racked our brains over the film's distribution problems. I suggested that we arrange its release in the USA ourselves by appointing an agent and renting the picture to universities and colleges on a one-day unlimited screening basis, and some time later this plan was put into action. It resulted in a very substantial box-office return in the order of $2 million – which just goes to prove that the young know best!

I now look back on *Magical Mystery Tour* with mixed feelings. It has clearly been an influence on a number of subsequent pop movies and comedies and, if Ian MacDonald is correct, can be seen as a forerunner to the road-movie genre that blossomed some two years later with *Easy Rider*. Paul has even suggested that it exerted an influence on the young Steven Spielberg, although I'm not quite sure how! At any rate it certainly includes some unique musical performances and remarkable sequences, none of which were replicated on film or video at any other time. So in many ways it is a film that I am happy to remember.

Of course, with more care the movie could have been several notches better than it was. To me, the 'Your Mother Should Know' sequence is a microcosm of all that is both good and bad about the film. The sets look great, the costumes look great, the music is great, the idea of placing the Beatles in a Busby Berkeley-style setting for a grand finale is great. Unfortunately the Beatles' dancing is bloody awful. It simply wasn't well enough rehearsed and fails to respect the technical perfection of the Hollywood musicals it pastiches. For me, the poor dancing undermines what would otherwise be a wonderful sequence, and every time I see it I think: If only you'd just taken the time to get it right; a few more minutes of rehearsal and it *would* have been right. But you can't unring a bell and *Magical Mystery Tour*, like any film, remains a permanent and unchangeable record of the decisions taken at the time it was shot and edited.

Frank Sinatra once said that he hated listening to his old records because he would hear all the little mistakes and regret that he was not sufficiently patient to rerecord them at the time. Fortunately for Frank, he was the only one who could hear them. But whenever I see *Magical Mystery Tour* I know just what he means.

So much for the start of Apple Films. There would be other opportunities and, as it turned out, *Magical Mystery Tour* eventually became very profitable. Alas, the same cannot be said for Apple Electronics and the Beatles' patronage of the Greek inventor 'Magic' Alexis Mardas.

After arriving in England as a student Alex was working as a television repairman for Olympic Electronics when he first came into contact with John Dunbar. Dunbar, a Cambridge graduate who had met Paul through Jane Asher's brother Peter, was a key conspirator in London's underground scene, having set up the Indica Gallery in 1966 with Peter Asher and Barry Miles. Dunbar had introduced Alex to the avant-garde art world and worked in partnership with him on the lighting for the European leg of the Rolling Stones' 1967 tour. Dunbar arranged the business and publicity, and Alex provided the electrical expertise. The Stones, however, were not overly impressed.

Alex first met John Lennon shortly after that tour through Dunbar, a mutual friend. Although Alex's knowledge of electronics was limited, he greatly impressed the Beatle, who swallowed many of his extravagant claims hook, line and sinker. Dubbed 'Magic' Alex by John, Mardas convinced him that all kinds of fantastical ideas and patents were possible if he were given the financial backing.

When John first introduced Alex to Paul, he apparently referred to him as 'my guru'. In a way John was easy prey for Alex. At the risk of being accused of applying cod psychology, I think that one of the consequences of John's boyhood losses was a desire to find leaders and guru figures. Moreover, John had always been fascinated by gadgetry but was a total layman as far as science and electronics were concerned. So when Alex told John that he would be able to build an invisible protective forcefield around his house, he was suitably impressed. Within a few short months Alex had ingratiated himself with the Beatles and become a close confidant of John's. In fact when John decided in late spring that the Beatles should escape from the pressures of fame by buying themselves an island, Alex came to the fore. He convinced John of his powerful family connections and persuaded him to look at the possibility of buying the Greek island of Leslo. That July he was instrumental in organizing a visit by the group to Greece to inspect it. Although the idea of buying the island was later dropped, it helped further to cement the relationship between Alex and John and, to some extent, him and the other Beatles.

A combination of the Beatles' gullibility and Alex's personal charm led the group to invest heavily in his extravagant inventions. In August 1967 it was agreed that he would become Head of Apple Electronics. He would be paid a good wage (according to Barry Miles, in *Many Years from Now*, around £40 a week) and 10 per cent of any profits from his inventions. Shortly after this he was set up in a workshop near London's Marylebone Station. From struggling television repairman to Apple executive and guru in a few short months was pretty good going, but it remained to be seen whether Alex could deliver on his promises? X-ray cameras, flying saucers, loudspeakers made of wallpaper, all manner of weird and wonderful ideas were mooted. Apple Electronics was set to become a centre of cutting-edge technology that would develop and patent the most revolutionary inventions imaginable and unimaginable.

Aside from the release of Paul's infectious 'Hello Goodbye' single, the other main project of late 1967 was the setting up and opening of the Beatles' Apple Boutique. Determined to diversify into other areas of business, the group commissioned the Dutch art collective The Fool to design exclusive clothes for their new Baker Street store. As a statement of intent The Fool also designed a huge psychedelic mural that was painted on to the shop front.

Simon Posthuma and Marijke Koger had first come to the UK in 1966, but it wasn't until 1967 that they, together with Josje Leeger, Barry Finch and businesss manager Simon Hayes, became involved with the Beatles. During that year they painted George's mini and, more famously, converted John's Rolls-Royce from a 'straight' status symbol into a psychedelic symbol of countercultural revolt. They worked on the inner sleeve of the *Sergeant Pepper* album and painted George's guitar and John's caravan. However, their most prestigious achievement came on 25 June 1967 when their psychedelically designed garments were donned by the Beatles and seen by some 400 million television viewers as the Beatles played 'All You Need Is Love' for the *Our World* satellite link-up. It sealed their reputation as the Beatles' exclusive couturiers and led directly to their ill-fated appointment as designers of the group's new boutique.

They had known for some time that the Beatles were looking to diversify, and Simon and Marijke had previously run a boutique in Amsterdam known as The Trend. The Beatles were receptive to their ideas, and it was agreed that they would be employed to create designs exclusively for the boutique which, alongside the garments, would also sell an assortment of Eastern knick-knacks, furniture, posters and underground books.

The kind of hippy attire that The Fool designed evoked the psychedelic whimsy of 1967. Inspired by the usual hippy sources (including ethnic Indian clothing, circus harlequins, dandyism and militaria) the kind of clothing that they produced – at great expense to the band – was first made available to the public after the boutique's grand opening Apple Juice Party on 5 December. Magic Alex had promised that for the grand opening he would set up an enormous free-standing electronic sun that would hover above the shop front and light up the building. It never happened, of course, and within a few short months the boutique at 94 Baker Street would be little more than a faded memory.

PART 2

The Apple's Core

5

Gurus, Gods and Gollum

APPLE MUSIC PUBLISHING had originally operated from a small office in Baker Street above the Apple Boutique, but by early 1968 it was clear that larger premises would be required for the master company. The new offices on Wigmore Street were located by Neil and chosen partly because EMI, their record label and soon-to-be distribution outlet for Apple Records, were situated close by.

On moving into Apple's new offices one of the first things I did was to have all the Beatles' legal documents shipped over from NEMS. The documents arrived in a state of disarray in numerous cardboard boxes. Most of them were not even filed. It was vital, however, that the group's legal agreements and business arrangements that had carried over from Brian's death be analysed properly. It was clear that we would need to employ a lawyer to take on this unenviable task, so I brought in a highly respected entertainment expert, Brian Lewis, to do just that.

Much of what we discovered was of little real significance. However, the investigation threw up one contract that might potentially have enormous impact on the Beatles' career. To our great surprise we discovered that the option for a third Beatles picture with United Artists had not been exercised. I do not remember the exact terms of the original contract, but the basis of the 1963–4 agreement was that the boys would make three films with United Artists. However, it was my opinion that the option on the contract had lapsed, and it was Queen's Counsel opinion that it was now null and void. Not that United Artists and Walter Shenson hadn't tried to make a third movie.

Throughout much of 1966 and 1967 they had done their utmost to find a new project that would interest the Beatles, even to the extent of hiring celebrated playwright Joe Orton to write a script in 1967. With a rise to fame that was almost as meteoric as the Beatles' own, Orton was earmarked by Walter as an ideal screenwriter for the group's next film. His highly successful stage plays, including *Loot* and *Entertaining Mr Sloane*, had taken the theatrical establishment by storm, and it was felt that his ribald, anarchic humour and acerbic wit would be a perfect foil for the Beatles' more gentle subversiveness. He was also a huge Beatles fan and was thrilled when a meeting was arranged with Paul. Orton's screenplay was called *Up Against It*, but it was never filmed because it was decided that its story – which included the Beatles appearing in drag, committing murder and going to prison – would do their image no favours. After paying Orton some £5,000 for the first draft, Walter and Brian agreed that they would have to look elsewhere, and the script was returned to him. He was angered that no reasons were given as to why his work had been rejected. This, however, was not the end of the story.

On 10 April 1967, just two days after the film was turned down by the Beatles' camp, it was bought by the famed producer Oscar Lewenstein for £10,000. Lewenstein, who was one of the heads of the highly successful British film production company Woodfall, felt that it was the most impressive first draft of any screenplay he had ever seen and was keen to forge ahead with an adaptation of the project that did not involve the Beatles. Woodfall had a track record that included the Oscar-winning *Tom Jones* and social realist movies of the calibre of *The Loneliness of the Long Distance Runner* and *A Taste of Honey*, and Orton had every right to feel that the company would do his screenplay full justice.

Ironically it was to the director of the first two Beatles films that Lewenstein turned as a potential director of the project. On 9 August 1967, shortly before I joined Apple, a meeting was arranged for Orton, Richard Lester and myself to discuss the production of the film. A car was sent from Twickenham studios to pick Orton up from his top-floor flat in Islington. There was no response when the chauffeur knocked at the door, and he called us at Twickenham to let us know.

I took the call. 'Try again,' I told him. 'He should be there.'

A few minutes later the chauffeur called again. He sounded in considerable shock, as he explained that after knocking three times he had looked through the letterbox and seen a man's body lying on the floor in the hallway; he was either dead or unconscious. The chauffeur didn't think it was Orton, as he had driven him before. From what he could make out the man on the floor appeared to be bald. My stomach churned. This sounded very bad.

'Leave this to me,' I told him and phoned Peggy Ramsay, Joe's theatrical agent, to tell her what had happened.

Orton's body was later recovered from the flat. He had been brutally murdered with a hammer by his lover Kenneth Halliwell, who had subsequently taken a lethal overdose of Nembutal and died in the hall. Orton was an atheist, and 'A Day in the Life' was played at his funeral. *Up Against It* was never made into a film, despite a number of posthumous rewrites by the cream of contemporary writers, including Charles Wood and Roger McGough.

As well as *Up Against It*, a number of other movie-related projects had been mooted around this time, and at one stage Walter had discussed the Beatles appearing in a film version of *The Three Musketeers*. There was also talk of making a musical version of Richard Condon's western *A Talent for Loving*. None of these ideas had come to anything, and we were now in a position to renegotiate the contract.

This was potentially wonderful news for the Beatles, since Brian had not negotiated a deal for the Beatles that reflected their enormous box-office potential. Part of this, I am sure, was because at the time when Brian first did his deal with United Artists he saw the cinema as a means of promoting the Beatles' records and maintaining their high profile rather than an end in itself. Also one has to remember that he had made the agreement just before the group had hit the peak of their popularity and before *A Hard Day's Night* had demonstrated the full extent of their bankability. Anyway, for whatever reason, the original deal had been very skewed in United Artists' favour and, despite some recognition of increasing percentages, certainly did not reflect the band's current status as the world's biggest celebrities.

I figured that if United Artists wanted to keep the Beatles – and, given their continued success, there was no reason why they wouldn't – they were going to have to renegotiate, and this time the odds would be stacked in our favour. I called David Chasman, then European Head of Production at United Artists, to discuss the situation. David and myself had always got on well, and we arranged to hold a formal meeting at his London office to review the lapsed contract. It was there that David realized the potential seriousness of the situation. Following our discussions, another meeting was arranged for the following February at United Artists' headquarters in New York. And this time it wouldn't be with just some major executive but with Arnold Picker, Company President, David Picker, Head of Production, and their Legal President. These were some of the most powerful men in the film business, and they were taking the situation very seriously indeed. It had the potential to be one of the most high-powered movie meetings of the decade. I set about preparing myself for it.

The Beatles knew nothing much about the gravity of the lapsed contract, although I did my best to keep them abreast of all developments affecting Apple Films. Meanwhile one of the first things they did jointly in 1968 was to take a trip down to Twickenham Studios to shoot a short live-action cameo sequence for their 'surprise' appearance at the end of a new cartoon film called *Yellow Submarine*. In fact, although it first reached the cinemas in 1968, its production genesis went way back to 1964.

During that year Brian was approached by a Hungarian-American cartoon producer, Al Brodax, whose company, King Features, wanted to make a series of short cartoon shows featuring the boys. Epstein and the Beatles eventually made an agreement with Brodax and so began, in September 1965, a series of around sixty children's cartoon shorts which were networked by the ABC network in the USA and not seen at all in the UK until many years after the Beatles had split up.

Looking back at the series today, it was probably just as well. It now seems incredibly trite. Made quickly and cheaply in the USA and London, the shorts are poorly executed and entirely witless, another unfortunate by-product of the mass commercialization of the group. Voiced by a mixture of American and British actors, the cartoon Beatles' accents bear no resemblance whatsoever to those of the real ones, and the plots of the shows are utterly ludicrous. But, like the souvenir merchandise that had boomed so successfully the previous year, they were astonishingly popular. For a while it seemed that the Beatles' name was the passport to profit – no matter how cheap or nasty the product.

Part of the original agreement between Brodax and Brian was that if the cartoon series proved successful Brodax would have the Beatles' blessing to make a feature film bearing their likeness and featuring a handful of original songs. When the series exceeded all expectations Brodax held Brian to his promise, and in 1967 production on the movie began in earnest.[1]

The film was to be directed by George Dunning, a Canadian animator with a vast range of experience, having worked successfully on commercials, avant-garde shorts and the US children's cartoon *The Gerald McBoing Boing Show*. The script of *Yellow Submarine*, which was based on the imagery of the Beatles' 1966 double A-side and popular *Revolver* LP track, was co-written by Brodax, Jack Mendelsohn, Lee Minoff and Erich Segal, a professor of Greek and Latin at Yale University who was later to write the screenplay for the hugely successful Oscar-winning movie *Love Story*. The film was funded by King Features and made in Britain through Dunning's TV Cartoons company for $1 million. It was an enormous project with contributions from some two hundred animators worldwide.

The Beatles were not at all keen on the project, feeling that it would undermine their newly acquired status as countercultural figureheads and social commentators. Having been deeply unimpressed by the initial cartoon series, I shared their doubts, until, that is, I saw how impressively the movie was developing. I then tried to persuade them to contribute their own voices to the soundtrack, but it was impossible to get them to agree to this: the cameo appearance was as far as they were prepared to go. They were adamant that they would have as little to do with the movie's production as possible, and, with the exception of four somewhat begrudgingly donated new songs and a few minor script ideas, contributed little to the film apart from their name. Like me, however, their attitude changed as they viewed more and more of the footage, and they were pleased with the finished result, giving the movie their seal of approval by turning up for the première at the London Pavilion on 17 July 1968.

The story pits the kindly animated Beatles against the wicked Blue Meanies, who seek to disrupt the happy karma of Pepperland. I think that part of the film's enduring appeal across the generations resides in the manner in which it offers itself up to a multiplicity of readings. For children, the simple narrative can be perceived as a modern fairy story in which the powers of love triumph over evil. It can also be read by more mature audiences as a fable that pits the forces of the underground against the overpowering oppressiveness of the establishment. After all, the script is brimming with sly references to Eastern mysticism, free love and hallucinogenic drugs which would not have been comprehensible to anyone younger than fifteen or sixteen.

Stylistically the movie epitomizes the audacious eclecticism of sixties pop-art styles. It assimilates a variety of influences from Bridget Riley's op art, Richard Hamilton's collages, Andy Warhol's silkscreen prints, the psychedelic poster art of Nigel Waymouth and Rick Griffin to Kandinsky's abstract expressionism and Salvador Dalí's surrealism.

This visual breadth is of course accompanied by an immensely ambitious range of film-making techniques, including conventional cel animation, rotoscoping and, of course, the live-action sequence at the film's closure. It was, quite simply, the single most ambitious piece of British animation ever undertaken. In retrospect, the film, released in July 1968, was historically important for a number of reasons.

First of all, the immense affability of the cartoon Beatles went quite some way to dispel the adverse effects of the bad publicity and controversy resulting from the *Magical Mystery Tour* fiasco and from Paul's pronouncements about his use of LSD.[2] Secondly, like the Bond films of the sixties, *Yellow Submarine* was an important precursor to today's multi-media blockbusters which, through tie-in merchandising, are designed to generate revenue in addition to box-office takings. In fact, the film was one of the first fully to realize the potential profits of associated products. Although movie merchandising was hardly new in 1968, the vast range of related items which the film generated (including alarm clocks, lunch-boxes, Corgi toy models and mobiles) formed an important blueprint for the multi-marketing spin-offs of such seventies productions as *Jaws* and *Star Wars*, a tradition which continues to this day. On a more positive note, the film was one of the first examples of a large-scale animation that successfully appealed to adults and children alike. It can be seen to anticipate the new wave of television animation comedies such as *The Simpsons*, *South Park* and the work of British Oscar winner Nick Park.

All of this is academic, however. For my money, *Yellow Submarine* exudes a quality sadly absent from many films today. That quality is charm. The Beatles were one of the best-loved pop groups of all time, but even they were rarely as lovable as their cartoon counterparts in *Yellow Submarine*. The film's utopian message that love can conquer evil has been much sneered at, as has John's song 'All You Need Is Love' which features in the film. This song has been attacked by a number of commentators as empty, simple-minded and sentimental sloganeering, the bland rhetoric of four supremely rich and pampered

85

pop stars. However, you have to have a very hard heart if you cannot enjoy the movie in the spirit in which it was made. It is, after all, the product of a different age. And, yes, it's simplistic, yes, it's idealistic, yes, it's sentimental. But is it possible for any film or song to appeal across such a wide generational divide and not have some of those qualities? And are they such negative ones anyway?

Having completed their minimal acting contributions for *Yellow Submarine*, the Beatles prepared for the release of their new single 'Lady Madonna'. Of all the Beatles' great innovations perhaps the most overlooked is their contribution to the development of the pop video, which they pioneered from 1965 onwards. Tired of flying all over the world to appear live on television pop shows, they or Brian (I don't know which) decided to produce a series of clips featuring the band miming to their most recent hits. These could be distributed internationally and save them the bother of having to travel from one television studio to another. Necessity, as they say, is the mother of invention, and at the time nobody realized the significance of this. Nobody anticipated that these short films or 'promo clips' would become the forerunners to the pop video; they were just a ruse to give the boys a bit more free time!

The first ten promo clips were shot by television director Joe McGrath in 1965 in just one day in a rented London studio.[3] But, as the Beatles' career progressed, their promos became increasingly ambitious and experimental in style, particularly the two shot by Swedish director Peter Goldmann for the 'Strawberry Fields'/'Penny Lane' single. By 1968 it was commonplace for each new Beatles single to have its own promo, and 'Lady Madonna' was no exception. I called my assistant, Tony Bramwell, and on Sunday 11 February arranged for us to shoot the Beatles miming to the track at Abbey Road Studios. When we arrived, however, things turned out differently. The group were on a roll as far as recording was concerned and didn't want to lose a day. Rather than mime for the promo film, they asked us instead to film them recording a new song they were working on at the time. The song, a forceful rock number written predominantly by John, was called 'Hey Bulldog', and that's the song that audiences saw in the clip. We tried to edit the footage so that it echoed the rhythm of 'Lady Madonna' (which wasn't too difficult since the songs have roughly similar tempos), but if you've ever wondered why that promo isn't lip-synched now you know!

'Lady Madonna' was one of the Beatles' strongest singles to date. Written mainly by Paul, it was the second successive McCartney song to grace a Beatles A-side. A forceful blues-and-boogie-inflected number complete with a great sax solo from the legendary Ronnie Scott, the single was in some ways a return to the more straightforward pop style of their pre-psychedelic days. It indeed proved something of a statement of intent, its musical and lyrical rootsiness signifying that the Beatles' flirtation with psychedelia in their words and music was now coming to an end.

The group's last single to be issued by Parlophone was backed by an equally memorable B-side, George's 'The Inner Light'. The instrumentation for George's prettiest piece of Eastern-style music thus far was recorded in India. It had initially been earmarked for inclusion on the soundtrack for *Wonderwall*, a 'swinging London' movie that starred Jack McGowran and which was directed by Joe Massot, who later went on to direct Led Zeppelin in their 1976 concert movie *The Song Remains the Same*. Although *Wonderwall* has since been consigned to the footnotes of sixties British cinema, George's soundtrack was the first official solo LP by a member of the group and featured some haunting instrumental snippets. I negotiated his involvement in the movie with Andrew Bronsberg, the film's producer. Although initially intended for the soundtrack LP, John and Paul were mightily impressed when, on George's return, they heard the song's lilting melody and decided to contribute the falsetto backing for George's lead vocals.

'The Inner Light' was a typically formidable Beatles B-side. Over the years much has been made of the fact that so few of the group's singles were issued on original LPs, but for me it is equally staggering that so many of their great flip-sides were not released on albums at the time. In fact, I believe that many of these were equal or, in some cases, superior in quality to the better-known songs they supported. 'This Boy', for example, has to stand as one of their most compelling early songs, as does Paul's mid-period rocker 'I'm Down', which, with its stellar performances and brutal delivery, was far more emotionally authentic than most of the material he contributed to the *Help!* LP. In fact, it's probably the most raw self-penned rock-and-roll song the Beatles ever committed to disc. Later B-sides would also prove to be of the very highest quality, and John's 'heavy' version of 'Revolution' and George's thunderous 'Old Brown Shoe' would, in my opinion, earn their place on any 'Best of' compilation. Similar sentiments can also be applied to the EP track 'Long Tall Sally', which, with Paul's earth-shattering vocal delivery, managed to give John's thunderous rendition of 'Twist and Shout' a run for its money.

By this point in 1968 the Beatles had become completely infatuated by the teachings of the Maharishi Mahesh Yogi, and on 16 February John and George flew out to join him in Rishikesh, north India, where they were to spend a prolonged period of time absorbing his teachings at his Meditation Academy. Paul and Ringo followed three days later. The Beatles' first brush with the Maharishi's theories on transcendental meditation took place on 24 August 1967, when John, Paul and George attended one of his lectures at the London Hilton in Park Lane. After the group's much-publicized visit to Bangor the following weekend, they were eager for a more sustained period of contact with the guru. So it seemed sensible for them to visit him on his own home turf, at his idyllic meditation school in the foothills of the Himalayas overlooking the sacred river Ganges.

I think there are several possible reasons why the group became interested in transcendental meditation and in the Maharishi's teachings. Sick of fandom and bored with drugs, the idea of peace and mental tranquillity was hugely appealing to a group of people who had realized all of their material ambitions but who found themselves wanting spiritually. What the Maharishi offered the Beatles was the ultimate sugar mountain: a belief system that would trade their outer turmoil for inner peace and which, when mastered, could be utilized at will at any time and in any situation.

Meanwhile back in London I was preparing for the meeting with United Artists about the Beatles' new film deal. I had had a good working relationship with the company in the past, and it seemed to make most sense to try to renegotiate more favourable terms with them than to take the Beatles' film deals elsewhere. As I saw it, John, Paul, George and Ringo were now the biggest stars in the world and I should attempt to negotiate a $1 million fee for each of them for any films they did with United Artists, if the company was interested in renewing the contract. The problem was that we didn't have a potential project or attached director to take to United Artists. I didn't have a script or option or even an idea for a screenplay that I could say that the Beatles wanted to make. Sure, we had thrown a few ideas around. From the beginnings of Apple we had done that, but nothing concrete had emerged, just strange and unworkable ideas like the Orton screenplay and the boys' short-lived plan to remake one of the Elvis pictures. Hal Kanter, who had written and directed the second Elvis film, *Loving You* and provided the screenplay for the hugely successful *Blue Hawaii*, had remained a good friend since we had worked together on a version of *A Midsummer Night's Dream* in Stratford-upon-Avon with Charles Laughton in 1961. I would have been delighted to work with Hal on a picture, but the suggestion was little more than a pipe dream that would have been both unworkable and retrograde.

Arriving at the St Regis Hotel in New York on the evening of 25 February I had no idea of what project to pitch to Arnold Picker the next day. Unable to sleep, I wracked my brains all night in a last-ditch attempt to come up with some kind of game-plan. And as I walked over to the United Artists offices for the meeting the following day I was resigned to the fact that their executives wouldn't entertain the idea of $1 million for each of the Beatles without a credible idea or proposal.

The meeting was taking place on the third floor. I walked through the front entrance and was just getting into the lift when, incredibly, an idea came to me. Like all good ideas it was deceptively simple. The new production from Apple Films would be a cinematic adaptation of one of the most popular and best-loved novels of the twentieth century, J.R.R. Tolkien's classic, *The Lord of the Rings*. It seemed to me to be a perfect project with which to interest United Artists and an ideal starting-point for the renegotiation of the Beatles' contracts.

There were many reasons why it made sense. Although it had been a huge seller, Tolkien's magnum opus had never been filmed, and I felt that its allusions to fantasy and mysticism would appeal greatly to the boys. Perhaps more importantly, the idea of the Beatles producing a score for the movie obviously fitted perfectly with the conceptual ambitions of *Sergeant Pepper* and *Magical Mystery Tour*.

The book's status would ensure a guaranteed youth audience, it having undergone a recent resurgence of interest with the arrival of hippy culture. And, while it would obviously be a huge undertaking to film, the concept had the grandiose, epic quality needed to justify the kind of deal that I was looking for. It's not every day that you get a truly great idea. It's not even every year. But, my God, you know damn well when you've just had one, and this was an absolute pearler! The only thing I had to do was to buy the film rights before the start of the meeting. I tried to remain calm and started to review my options.

I entered the United Artists offices and asked if I could have a couple of minutes to make a private call. I called Jack Schwartzman, an old friend and business colleague in California who specialized in industry law and the acquisition of film rights. I told him my idea and asked if the rights were available but was told that he had recently acquired them on behalf of another producer. This was bad news.

'OK, Jack, I'll give whoever owns them whatever they paid plus $100,000 profit on top.'

'Sorry, Denis. I can't sell them.'

A hundred thousand profit was a serious amount of money to turn down so dismissively. It meant, without a doubt, that the rights had been bought by a major film distributor.

'Who's got them?'

'You know I can't tell you that.'

This was very tricky, but I had to find some way to ascertain their ownership.

'OK, Jack. You can't tell me who's got them, but you can tell me who's *not* got them!'

There was a brief silence while he considered this. Finally, and to my great relief, he agreed that to do this was not, at least directly, betraying the confidence of his clients. 'I suppose I can do that' was his somewhat reluctant response, and I proceeded to name all the majors that might have shown an interest in the book.

'Warner Brothers?'

'No.'

'Paramount?'

'No.'

'Columbia?'

'No.'

'Universal?'

'No.'

'United Artists?'

Silence.

'Thanks, Jack.'

I went into the meeting and explained to Arnold and David Picker about the lapsed contracts. I told them that we would be prepared to renew them for a film in which the Beatles were paid $1 million each. I told them that the film we wanted to make was *Lord of the Rings*, a book they already owned. There was a deathly silence, followed by a short period in which David and Arnold conferred in private with one other.

When they returned, David confirmed that they did indeed have the rights to *Lord of the Rings* and told me I was the only European producer that they would be prepared to entrust with such a project. I was flattered by his remarks. The proviso, however, would be that United Artists would consider the project only if I could get a major director involved in the project. We agreed, and I gave him a shortlist of names. These included David Lean, Michelangelo Antonioni and Stanley Kubrick. I left the offices in a state of pure elation. Now I just had to get the Beatles and a major director interested in the film and we would be away!

My first choice for the film was David Lean, director of the epics *Lawrence of Arabia*, *Bridge on the River Kwai* and *Dr Zhivago*. With some of the most successful and critically respected movies of all time to his credit, he had a formidable track record and his seniority, I thought, would make him an ideal father figure to the Beatles. Another advantage, I figured, was that I knew that he had considerable respect for the group's music and, indeed, their previous films, particularly *A Hard Day's Night*. I had met him on several occasions at various movie-related events, and whenever we talked he mentioned his admiration for the film, particularly the multi-camera shooting technique that Richard had employed. On returning to the hotel I telephoned him in Ireland, where he was starting pre-production on a new movie. He sounded happy to hear from me again. I explained the project to him and told him why I thought he would be the ideal director for the film.

'It's a very interesting idea, Denis,' he told me. 'Unfortunately I'm tied up at the moment with a little love story I'm going to do out here.'

The 'little love story' turned out to be *Ryan's Daughter* and, sadly, that was the end of his involvement in the project.

The next person I needed to get hold of was Stanley Kubrick. This caused me some trepidation, since my only previous contact with him had been over the *Mystery Tour* footage, and film industry lore had it that he could be reclusive, distant and difficult to deal with. You certainly didn't just call him out of the blue; you had to have some kind of intermediary, a go-between who could set up a discussion or meeting. Fortunately in my friend James B. Harris I had just such a person. Jimmy had produced *Dr Strangelove* for Kubrick some five years earlier, and I knew him through *The Bedford Incident*, which he directed and I produced. I called him, and he kindly agreed to arrange for me to speak to Kubrick.

Despite the director's formidable reputation I found him both polite and charming when I spoke to him on the telephone. The only problem was that he was not familiar with the Tolkien books; given their popularity and the critical respect accorded to them, I found this surprising. I told him that we were very interested in getting him involved and that I would send the books round to him so he could take a look at them. He told me that the next day he would be sailing back from the USA to the UK, and I arranged for the trilogy to be delivered to his cabin on the liner, telling him that it would make excellent reading for the Atlantic crossing. I thanked him and hung up. Minutes later he called me back to inform me that his daughter had just berated him for never having read the books and told him that he should be ashamed to admit to anyone that he didn't know about them. We laughed and agreed to speak again once he had had a chance to read them and consider the project. Things looked very positive indeed.

On returning from New York I knew that I had to keep up the momentum. Unfortunately the Beatles were still in India and not really in the mood to talk business. I felt that the only way to interest them in the film would be to get them all together and to tell them what I had in mind and the situation with United Artists. I decided that if they didn't return to England soon I would fly out to India to discuss the project with them in person. This was, after all, potentially a huge deal.

However, just as I was weighing up whether to go, the decision was taken for me. One morning in early March I received a telegram from the Beatles asking me to join them to work on a film about transcendental meditation. I was perplexed, as nobody had mentioned anything about this to me before and I couldn't understand who was behind the idea. I didn't much like the sound of it, but the trip would represent an ideal opportunity to discuss *The Lord of the Rings*, so I was more than happy to fly out. Neil had also been summoned by the boys. They wanted him to update them on how other aspects of their business had been progressing, so we travelled together.

At the end of the tiring long-haul flight we touched down in the blistering heat of New Delhi before boarding the ancient Ambassador car that had been sent from Rishikesh for the final phase of the journey. This was an event in itself. The car was a rickety old banger that felt as if it would give up the ghost at any moment, and the driver did not seem to know where he was going, at one point getting hopelessly lost and putting an extra thirty miles on to what was already a considerable distance over bumpy and potholed roads. At one point, about halfway through what must have been the most uncomfortable 150-mile drive of my life, we were halted by an official road-block manned by three or four policemen and a doctor. We got out of the car and, while Neil went for a stroll by a nearby canal, the policemen examined my passport. I was informed that I had to have an injection, although it was impossible to ascertain what it was for. I didn't want any trouble, so I let them inject me with whatever it was they had in their hypodermic syringes. Fortunately there weren't any unpleasant side-effects.

I was aware of the grip that the Maharishi had on the boys at the time, but it wasn't until I arrived in Rishikesh that I realized the full extent of John's and George's infatuation with his ideas. Ringo, on the other hand, wasn't really cut out for transcendental meditation, and it turned out that the most down-to-earth member of the band was leaving just as we arrived. Neil and I were to move into his bungalow.

After gathering up all his bits and pieces Ringo came over and smiled laconically. 'Denis, I've left you a present behind the door.'

Very nice, I thought, and almost immediately forgot all about it. When, after a communal evening meal of unidentifiable vegetation, I returned to the room I found dozens of tins of Heinz baked beans stacked up on the window ledge. Having just sampled the Maharishi's cuisine I was genuinely grateful!

'Goodfellas!'
Left to right: Brian Epstein, Dick Van Dyke, Walter Shenson,
Mal Evans, Alun Owen and me at Twickenham Studios

© Denis O'Dell

With Walter Shenson, producer of *A Hard Day's Night* and *Help!*
© Denis O'Dell

Paul's father Jim McCartney with his
racehorse Drake's Drum

© Denis O'Dell

With Richard Lester,
director of *A Hard Day's Night*

© Denis O'Dell

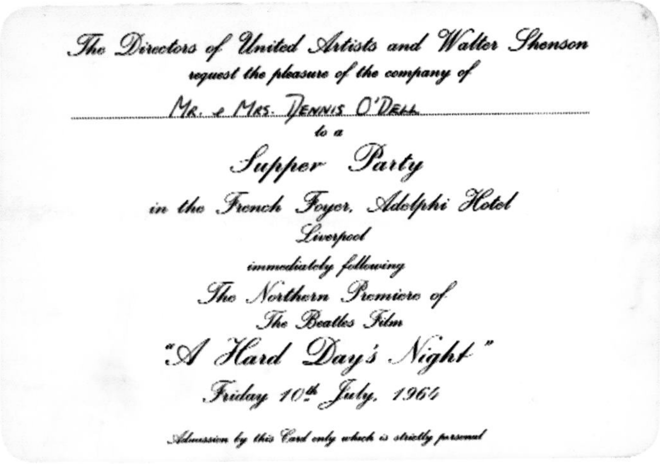

The Directors of United Artists and Walter Shenson
request the pleasure of the company of

MR. & MRS. DENNIS O'DELL

to a

Supper Party

in the French Foyer, Adelphi Hotel
Liverpool
immediately following
The Northern Premiere of
The Beatles Film
"A Hard Day's Night"
Friday 10th July, 1964

Admission by this Card only which is strictly personal

Invitation to the United Artists party following the northern première
of *A Hard Day's Night*

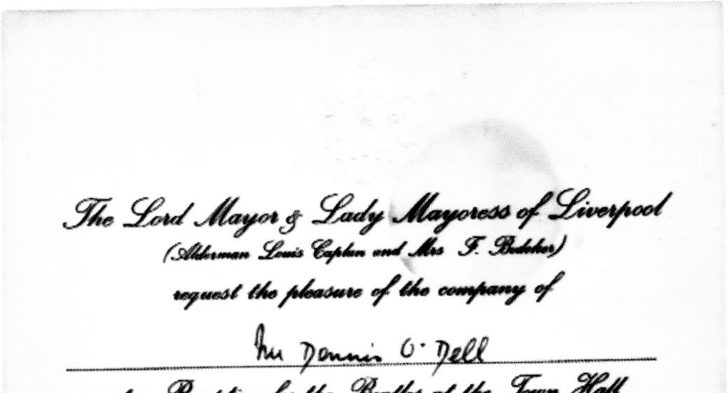

The Lord Mayor & Lady Mayoress of Liverpool
(Alderman Louis Caplan and Mrs F. Bidoloer)
request the pleasure of the company of

Mr Dennis O'Dell

at a Reception for the Beatles at the Town Hall
on Friday, 10th July, 1964, from 7 p.m. to 8 p.m.

Dress optional
R.S.V.P. on the
enclosed card not later
than 1st July, 1964

Admission tickets will be issued
after the acceptance of this
invitation.

Invitation to the reception of the Liverpool première
of *A Hard Day's Night*

Nic Roeg and me in San Francisco
on the set of *Petulia*, starring
George C. Scott and Julie Christie
© *Denis O'Dell*

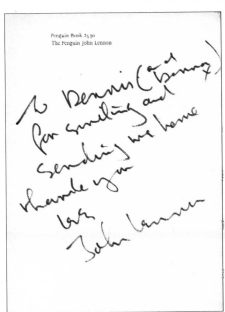

Above: John's lovely inscription inside *The Penguin John Lennon* expressing his relief at being allowed to leave Spain at the end of the shooting of *How I Won the War* in 1966

Below: My son Shaun's gift from John

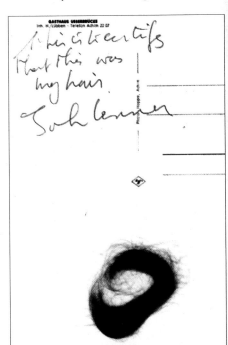

At the Apple's core . . .
Back row, left to right: Mal Evans,
Magic Alex, Ron Kass, Brian Lewis,
Derek Taylor and me

Front row, left to right:
Paul, John and Neil Aspinall
A good beginning . . .

Above: With John and Paul, launching
Apple at the Americana Hotel,
New York, 1968

© Denis O'Dell

Below: With Paul for the inaugural
meeting aboard the Chinese junk,
New York, 1968

© Denis O'Dell

Surely a golden apple!

© Denis O'Dell

All aboard!
John, Mal and Derek
on the Chinese junk
© Denis O'Dell

With Mary Hopkin,
a key Apple artist
© Denis O'Dell

Godparents Neil Aspinall and Nic Roeg at my son Arran's christening in 1968; the character in the middle is probably a gatecrasher!

© Denis O'Dell

The note that turned up on my desk prior to the making of the 'Hey Jude' video

With George Harrison in 1969
© *Denis O'Dell*

With Paul and Linda in 1969
© Denis O'Dell

With Peter Sellers
aka Sir Guy Grand
© Denis O'Dell/Grand Films

Above: With Ringo on the first day of shooting for *The Magic Christian*
© Denis O'Dell/Grand Films

Below: Ringo discusses his role in *The Magic Christian* as
Youngman Grand with writer Terry Southern
© Denis O'Dell/Grand Films

Above: Arriving at Twickenham
Studios with Peter Sellers,
Ringo Starr and Princess
Margaret during the shooting
of *The Magic Christian*
© *Denis O'Dell/Grand Films*

Right: Peter Sellers discusses
the film with Princess Margaret.
© *Denis O'Dell/Grand Films*

Princess Margaret, a friend of Peter Sellers,
visited the set of *The Magic Christian*.
© *Denis O'Dell/Grand Films*

Preparing to shoot the galley-slave
sequence for *The Magic Christian*
© *Denis O'Dell/Grand Films*

Above: With Paul, Linda, Ringo and Maureen at the launch party of *The Magic Christian*
© *Denis O'Dell/Grand Films*

Right: Life's a gamble! The bank notes weren't real, by the way.
© *Denis O'Dell/Grand Films*

Royal World Premiere

in the presence of
HRH The Princess Margaret,
Countess of Snowdon
in aid of the
National Society for the
Prevention of
Cruelty to Children

Commonwealth United Presents a Grand Film Starring
Peter Sellers & Ringo Starr in The Magic Christian
Also starring WILFRID HYDE WHITE • ISABEL JEANS • CAROLINE BLAKISTON with guest stars RICHARD ATTENBOROUGH
LEONARD FREY • LAURENCE HARVEY • CHRISTOPHER LEE • SPIKE MILLIGAN
Produced by DENIS O'DELL Directed by JOSEPH McGRATH Executive Producers HENRY T. WEINSTEIN & ANTHONY B. UNGER
Screenplay by TERRY SOUTHERN & JOSEPH McGRATH from the novel by TERRY SOUTHERN
Colour by TECHNICOLOR Released by COMMONWEALTH UNITED ENTERTAINMENT (UK) LTD. Music by KEN THORNE

Odeon Theatre, Kensington, Thursday 11th December 1969, 7.00 pm for 8.10 pm

KINDLY BE SEATED BY 8.10 p.m.   ROYAL CIRCLE 25 gns.
A35
DRESS: BLACK TIE

Above: Donna and I
meeting Princess Margaret
with Joe McGrath and Peta
at the Royal Première of *The
Magic Christian* and my
invitation to the British
première of the film
© Denis O'Dell/Grand Films

Left: John and Yoko at the
première of *The Magic
Christian* protesting at the
execution of James Hanratty
© Denis O'Dell/Grand Films

Below: A birthday card from Ringo,
who was also the artist

Above: A photo from the *QE2* given
to Donna by Ringo in 1969

Ringo with Maureen and family
on board the *QE2*
© *Denis O'Dell*

Above: Dinner at the Las
Vegas International with,
among others, Joe McGrath
and Ringo Starr. This was
taken the night we saw Elvis
perform there.
© *Denis O'Dell*

Right: The signed menu
acquired from our Las Vegas
trip with Ringo

With Richard Lester on the set of *Royal Flash*
in the mid-seventies

© *Denis O'Dell*

With Richard Lester in the
mid-seventies
© Denis O'Dell

With Sean Connery on the set of
Robin and Marian
© Denis O'Dell

The self-portrait that John left on my desk

6

Twilight of the Gods

THE ATMOSPHERE AT the Academy of Transcendental Meditation was extremely tranquil. Everything seemed to move in a kind of sun-drenched slow motion. The three remaining Beatles, along with other suitably attired celebrity acolytes such as Mike Love of the Beach Boys, Donovan and sisters Mia and Prudence Farrow, attended seminars with the guru at various intervals throughout the day but also spent many hours in deep private meditation. In fact, so impressed was I with the three Beatles' devotion to the Maharishi's teachings that I, too, attended his seminars and spent many hours meditating with them. The school, or ashram, was situated on a flat plain in the foothills of the Himalayas above the Ganges and was surrounded on both sides by jungle. Access to the school was via a suspension bridge that crossed the river from the relatively small and undeveloped town of Rishikesh. There was also a boat service that ferried people across.

While extremely simple by the Beatles' standards, the accommodation wasn't totally primitive. There was hot running water, and the little bungalows that we shared were carpeted and furnished with four-poster beds, chairs and tables. The academy was also well served by at least thirty staff employed by the Maharishi to take care of the cleaning, cooking, gardening and general upkeep. Near the row of bungalows was the lecture theatre and an indoor dining-room, which I cannot recall being used since the weather was fine for the duration of our stay. Instead, we tended to eat communally in a space that was partially walled by glass to keep greedy monkeys from gaining access and grabbing all the food.

Even though it was described variously as a 'school' or an 'academy', there was no rigorous discipline. The idea was that the students should learn at their own pace and conduct their meditation for the length of time and with the degree of intensity that they felt appropriate for them. A typical day began with a communal breakfast, although no set times were ever specified, so people would drop in and out of the dining area all morning. The bulk of the day would then consist of meditation or simply lazing about and chatting to the other guests, reading or, in the Beatles' case, composing songs. Some people would meditate in their rooms and would not be seen for many hours at a time. Others would be less solitary. The Maharishi would make himself available for some of the time, although mostly he would be meditating himself. We weren't entirely left on our own, however, since the Maharishi had a trusted aide, Bramacharya Rhaghwendra, who was available throughout the day to advise on our spiritual development. Twice each day, once in the afternoon and once in the evening, we would attend lectures at which we were encouraged to tell the Maharishi how we were progressing. Evenings would consist of another communal vegetarian meal usually attended by all the students.

I found him a tremendously warm man and a gifted instructor, and being exposed to his teachings made me realize why the Beatles had become so enamoured with him. He seemed to radiate goodwill, peace and wisdom. Given the stressful time I was having in the UK sorting out the band's tangled business affairs and after the critical mauling of *Magical Mystery Tour* the meditation classes came at a fortuitous time for me, too, despite the fact that I had ostensibly come out to India to talk business.

Although I never became what you might call a convert to Eastern mysticism and did not meditate on a regular basis after leaving the ashram, the time I spent with the Maharishi certainly had a profound effect on me at the time. In fact I am sure that learning the basics of his meditation technique helped to relieve what was becoming an increasingly stressful lifestyle. What cannot be doubted is that meditation is a powerful and positive tool that can have genuinely life-enhancing effects on anyone who experiences it. The Maharishi personally gave me a mantra, and I still treasure the two books that he gave me as a gift, his tract on meditation, *The Science of Being and the Art of Living*, and his translation of the *Bhagavad-Gita*. He signed both, but I particularly liked the inscription he wrote on the fly-sheet of the latter: 'The song of life sung by the lord is to be sung, dear blessed Denis O'Dell, so that the echo sings for generations to come!' A bit flowery and fanciful, perhaps, but gracious words from a great spiritual leader. And like all spiritual leaders, his tongue was every bit as silvery as his beard!

The strangest memory I have of India occurred shortly after I arrived, probably on the second or third day. During the afternoon George approached me and explained that since he had been in India he had developed the ability to levitate. I was aware of his extreme devotion to transcendental meditation but was taken aback by this extraordinary statement. To my utter amazement, however, he proceeded to lay down in his room and attempted to demonstrate this remarkable new ability. I watched, transfixed, for what seemed like hours but in reality was probably only a few short minutes. To this day I am not sure whether or not he succeeded. I remember thinking that maybe his body did rise two or three inches, although I honestly can't say for sure. One thing is certain. If anybody was capable of such a thing it was George. He was – and, I believe, remained – a devout believer in the power of meditation.

The harmony was not to last of course, John eventually becoming particularly disenchanted with the Maharishi and suspicious of his motives. Much has been made of the allegedly 'dishonest' and 'corrupting' nature of the Maharishi, and he was later ridiculed by the Beatles themselves in the words of John's thinly veiled character assassination 'Sexy Sadie' (the original title, 'Maharishi', was changed at the eleventh hour to avoid possible litigation), where he is denounced as a false prophet, a confidence trickster on the make who used the Beatles to increase his financial and spiritual empire. Yet while it is probably fair to say that the Maharishi saw the Beatles' association with him as a means to further his own organizational and commercial ends, it is important to remember that it was the Beatles who approached him in the first place. Moreover, it has often been suggested that the group grew disenchanted with the Maharishi after they became suspicious that he had seduced one of the women in his entourage at the ashram. This may be true, but, as far as I am aware, the rumours that were at the heart of any accusations were exaggerated at best and pure fiction at worst. John's bitter disenchantment with his guru was, I think, born more out of having had his illusions shattered when he realized that 'Sexy Sadie' was ultimately no more than a gifted meditation teacher, for all the mysticism he espoused.

When they were not practising meditation the Beatles played their guitars on the roofs of their bungalows, strumming the compositions that would eventually make up much of the 'White Album'. I didn't fully appreciate it at the time, but it was a great privilege to have been so close to them at such a private period in their career and to witness them composing some of their most memorable songs at such close quarters. What was fascinating for me was their sheer musicality, particularly in the case of John and Paul. Wonderful and enchanting melodies seemed to flow effortlessly from them, as though they were the involuntary channels for some supreme musical power source. This sounds ridiculous, of course, but the whole process of artistic creation is fundamentally mystical and when they were composing it was as if they were incapable of writing songs that were not beautifully crafted. They seemed able to tap into any musical style they chose, stamping their own imprint on it and in the process somehow making it their own. Lyrically they were also incredibly astute, often taking their inspiration from the moment, some seemingly trivial or inconsequential personal incident or event that they would somehow manage to universalize.

The most famous example of this is John's song 'Dear Prudence'. After being impressed at a lecture in the USA by the Maharishi in January 1968, Mia and Prudence Farrow had decided to study at the Maharishi's academy. Both of them got on well with the Beatles, so when Prudence became deeply depressed and refused to emerge from her room John wrote the song to try to coax her out. The song, which had a childlike charm all of its own, was a plea for her to forget whatever it was that was depressing her and to take pleasure in her surroundings and in her companions. It was an earnest, folky song that somehow managed to transcend its original inspiration and be transformed into an anthem to self-discovery and spaced-out optimism. I watched as John and George walked over to Prudence's bungalow, sat down outside and John played the song on his acoustic guitar. I would like to be able to say that Prudence emerged, but, despite what some rather more fanciful accounts have claimed, that isn't what happened. There wasn't any kind of miracle, and Prudence didn't come out to play. In fact, for all I know she may have been in a state of such deep meditation or depression that she barely heard the song. All I can say is that she did start to come out of her depressive trance in the next few days, and I'm sure that John's song didn't do any harm. I'm just pleased that John realized what a fine composition it was and retained it for the Beatles to incorporate into the new album.

This LP was *The Beatles* or the 'White Album', as it was rechristened by fans on its release some nine months later in November 1968. It has, perhaps more than any other Beatles LP, become the subject of the most critical scrutiny and controversy. Was it their greatest piece of work or their weakest? A masterwork that gels together seamlessly or a patchwork of disconnected and half-baked ideas?

The jury is still out, but, for what it's worth, I think it is one of the Beatles' greatest achievements. For me, it's the most challenging record the group ever released, embracing a wider musical panorama than had been attempted before or since in pop. The diversity of the LP is remarkable in its ambition, embracing and pastiching virtually every musical genre of the twentieth century with panache, energy and wit.

George Martin and a number of critics have claimed that it would have been better if scaled down to a single album. But what would they remove? While it is true to an extent that the album is greater than the sum of its parts, it includes some remarkable songs (songs such as Paul's 'Blackbird' and John's 'Goodnight' are fast becoming standards, while 'Happiness Is a Warm Gun' is a remarkably ambitious piece). That said, the overall quality of the LP resides in its sheer breadth. Whatever else it may be, the 'White Album' is the Beatles' most convincing testament to their love and understanding of an extraordinary range of musical styles and, in tracks such as 'Helter Skelter', their desire to create new ones. In my opinion, no modern pop LP has looked backwards more affectionately or forward so bravely as the 'White Album'.

It is a shame that so many contemporary British bands seem to use the Beatles as their main influence in their compositions and production, constantly trying to recreate the acid-soaked sound of *Revolver*-era Beatles. What is the point? With the 'White Album' the Beatles proved their ability to look beyond their own immediate rock-and-roll heritage, and modern pop, if it is to progress with integrity, needs to do the same. In fact, if anything, slavish copying of the Beatles' music and image is, in a way, the most misguided tribute to them imaginable, since it represents everything they were not about. The 'White Album' remains a milestone of what can be achieved in pop, but the Beatles need to be regarded more as an example than a model and perhaps respected a little less than they have been in the past few years. After all, if popular music is to remain interesting, musicians need to realize that holding any one style in too much reverence is not healthy. It is the enemy of vitality, change and development.

Of all the Beatles it was clear that George, as the most interested in the Maharishi's teachings, was mostly behind getting me out to India to discuss the transcendental meditation film project. I understood the Beatles' desire to promote the Maharishi's ideas, but I could not envisage how a subject as inherently introverted, internalized and spiritual as meditation could translate itself visually into a successful feature film or documentary. The idea seemed to me to be utterly self-defeating anyway, since the only obvious audience would be people who were already initiates, and they didn't need to be convinced of its benefits. Matters were also complicated by the fact that another production company, Bliss Productions, was in the process of arranging a documentary with the Maharishi and, although Bliss wanted the Beatles to appear in the film, they would have second billing to the guru, so there would be a clear clash of interests over control. I also knew that United Artists would never accept such a project as a third film and told them so. I then started to introduce my idea of making a film version of *The Lord of the Rings*. I had brought copies of the books with me and with a little help from Donovan – long an ardent admirer of Tolkien – persuaded John, Paul and George to take a look at the trilogy. Rather than each having to read the books from cover to cover, each was given one of the books. Paul read the first, *The Fellowship of the Ring*, John read *The Two Towers* and George *The Return of the King*.

Fortunately the meditation project began to take a back seat as Paul, John and George became increasingly enthused about the possibilities of a musical film of the Tolkien trilogy. The three Beatles were truly inspired by the idea, each beginning to earmark roles for themselves.[1] John was keen to play Gandalf and was so enthusiastic that he told me it would be no problem to get 'at least a double album' of musical material together for the project. For once, it seemed, at least three of the Beatles had reached an agreement about a film they all wanted to do. And when Paul and myself decided to return to London, leaving John and George in India, I really did believe that after the

103

disappointment of *Magical Mystery Tour* we were finally on to a winner. I saw the film as a massive project that would exploit and stretch the Beatles' screen-acting potential, expand their musical horizons and elevate them into the world's biggest box-office stars.

On returning to the UK I called Stanley Kubrick to determine his response to the books I had sent him. I hoped that he would have been sufficiently taken by them to make the film with us. To my great surprise and disappointment, however, he told me that he thought the books, while extraordinary, were 'unmakable'. This, I felt, was a remarkable statement coming from one of the industry's great visionaries. I told him so and said that, in my opinion, there was no such thing as an unfilmable book. I urged him to reconsider and persuaded him to at least meet John and Paul to discuss the project in more depth, and he agreed. Following John's return, I arranged a business lunch for the three of them at the old MGM studios at Borehamwood but decided not to attend myself. Kubrick knew my feelings about the film, and I felt it best for the meeting to take place in as casual an atmosphere as possible.

Since I wasn't there I don't know exactly what was said. What I do know is that afterwards the Beatles lost all interest in the project, so I can only assume that Kubrick dissuaded them of its cinematic potential. In a last-ditch effort to interest him I called him again a few days after the meeting with John and Paul, but he was adamant that the film could not be made. He was very civil about it but was unshakeable in his conviction that it was not a challenge that he or any other director could pull off. He then went on to ask me if I would be interested in leaving Apple and joining him to produce a film version of the life of Napoleon. I was sorely tempted!

So that was that. I suppose, in retrospect, that not getting to make *The Lord of the Rings* represents the biggest disappointment of my time at Apple. To this day I still think it had great potential and could have been a truly extraordinary movie. Of course, it was eventually made into an animated feature in the late seventies, although I felt it was a weak adaptation and nothing like the film I had in mind. But I remain of the opinion that there is no such thing as a film that cannot be made. I must admit that I smiled wrily to myself when I found out that thirty-two years later it has been made into a series of highly successful feature films, the first of which is currently breaking all box office records. I'm looking forward to seeing them immensely . . . I think!

7

The Big Apple

By MID-1968 Apple was well established. As well as the films, electronics and clothing ventures, the record department had now begun in earnest and there were all manner of subdivisions. The Wigmore Street offices were now really up and running. The premises themselves were fairly uninspiring, just a huge floor of rented office space which, beyond an open-plan reception area, housed the Beatles and the Apple staff and executives. But for all of their apparent ordinariness and respectability, the goings-on therein were a constant source of intrigue, enjoyment and good-natured mischief. The reception area, for example, was always worth a visit, as one never knew who would be next to stroll through the doors. The building became a magnet for the famous and infamous, the strange and the exotic, the eccentric and the odd. One never could tell what would happen next. One of my oddest and happiest memories occurred in the early Wigmore Street days, not long after we had moved into the building in January. I was presiding over one of the rare board meetings with Neil, Peter Brown and numerous others including Paul, who was, typically, the only Beatle to attend. Although Apple was ostensibly their company, it was almost impossible by this time to get all four members of the group together in one room at the same time. The Beatles loathed business meetings, and Paul was the only one who actively made an effort to turn up. As I recall, this particular meeting had been called to discuss the future of the recently opened Apple Boutique.

At the time my wife Donna was in a London hospital, heavily pregnant with our son Arran. We were midway through what was turning into a pretty tense meeting when a phone call came through to the boardroom. Paul, who was sitting next to the phone, took the call and the room went quiet while he briefly spoke to the caller. Putting down the phone, he turned to me.

'Congratulations, Denis,' he said and turned to address everybody in the room. 'While you lot have all been sitting around doing absolutely nothing and getting absolutely nowhere, Denis's wife has just done something useful and given birth to a son.'

I was elated. And Neil Aspinall, who had become a close friend, kindly agreed to become Arran's godfather. Some months later, when Paul was visiting at our house, we were sitting in the living-room talking babies, and Donna and I mentioned that Arran's birth had been a difficult one and that he had eventually been delivered via Caesarean section. Paul stood up and walked over to Donna, who had Arran on her knee, and carefully picked him up, looking deep into his eyes.

'Well,' said Paul, 'you don't want to worry about that, you know. Babies born that way are usually more intelligent.'

'I didn't know that,' I told him.

'Oh yes, and I should know,' he said, smiling. 'I was one!'

As well as having an office, I took another room and started putting together a library of Beatles-related film and video performances. I was shocked that there was no archive already in existence and felt it was essential to collect and file all the old promo clips, newsreels and other appearances for future reference. Neil saw the sense in this, and we soon found we had an array of Beatles footage, neatly racked and filed in numbered round film cans. As well as housing archival footage, the cans also had a secondary function for the boys, who used them as a hiding place for whatever drugs they were into at the time – usually cannabis. They would hide their stash in a numbered can and if, for example, they were over at Abbey Road recording and required some extra stimulation they would send someone round to collect the appropriately numbered container. The numbers would, of course, be changed regularly.

The archive proved a sensible and astonishingly profitable idea. Much of the material we put together was later edited by Neil into the rough cut of a film called *The Long and Winding Road*. Sadly, the movie was never completed in its intended form. However, much of the footage we collected eventually surfaced in the hugely successful documentary series the *Beatles Anthology* in 1996.

The archive was not the only early idea I had that turned out to be immensely profitable. As I have mentioned, top earners in late sixties Britain were incredibly heavily taxed, and I was always trying to come up with ways of legitimately expanding the Beatles' empire and maximizing profits. A suggestion that I came up with soon after the formation of the company was to register and copyright the Apple companies and the Apple name in as many different territories worldwide as we could for the distribution of all Apple product. The reason for this was twofold. First, it would ensure the official 'branded' status of Apple as an organization and prevent others from fraudulently trading off our name, which, as far as merchandising was concerned, was something that had cost the Beatles dearly in the past. I also felt that such a move would enhance the prospect of acquiring international talent. I talked all this through with Neil, and he agreed we should go ahead. This turned out financially to be the single most important financial idea that I had for the Beatles – or at least for their legacy. The copyrighting of the Apple name meant millions for their enterprise with the rise of companies such as Apple computers and the resulting settlements that they had to pay for the continued use of the name. I was unaware of this until some twenty-three years after the group disbanded, when at one of my birthday parties Neil told me that my original idea currently brought in around £1 million a year for Apple. It's a pity that they didn't ask me to share in this windfall!

In keeping with Paul's original philanthropic ideals, the Beatles decided to place an advertisement in the music papers and on street posters asking young hopefuls and would-be musicians to submit demo tapes to the company. Largely masterminded by Paul in April 1968, the poster featured Alistair Taylor, Apple's office manager, dressed as a busker in one-man-band garb. The accompanying caption informed readers that the man in the picture now owned a Bentley and that they could, too, if they sent in their tapes to the company. An avalanche of unlistenable drivel subsequently bombarded the organization and, although Apple did discover and successfully promote a good deal of new talent, including James Taylor, Mary Hopkin and Badfinger, none arrived as a result of the advertising campaign.

The Wigmore Street offices now contained a variety of weird and wonderful characters. I recall them all with affection. Peter Brown, originally an assistant of Brian Epstein's, became an Apple executive after helping to run the Beatles' affairs following Brian's death. Suave and charming, he was a great diplomat and an ideal person to talk to if you wanted feedback on any ideas you had in the pipeline. Ron Kass, who had been an executive at Liberty Records, was a fastidious, elegant and somewhat eccentric man and very good at his job. He spent a great deal of his time at Apple travelling and establishing branches of the record label throughout the world. His office was pristine white with no desk, just a huge white drawing-board where, in almost military style, he would chart Apple Records' plans for world domination. He was married to Joan Collins for some years, and, sadly, he died of cancer in the mid-eighties.

Alistair, another of Brian's original employees, also became a permanent fixture at Apple. Likeable, efficient and willing to please, he became an excellent general office manager, the Beatles' 'Mr Fix-It', who did his best to accommodate the group's day-to-day requirements and requests.

The award for the oddest appointment at Apple has to go to Caleb, the tarot reader and I-Ching thrower, who also became involved briefly in the running of the Apple Boutique. First and foremost, however, he was Apple's in-house mystic. John, as I've mentioned, was particularly fascinated by mystics and people with 'magical' abilities, and Caleb fitted the bill perfectly. I don't know how he came to be involved with the Beatles or what his background was, but mystics are rarely keen to disclose too much about themselves, and most sixties gurus had an acute fear of exposing the ordinariness of their lives that could undermine their cosmic auras. For all I know, Caleb's real name may have been Nigel or Graham and when he disrobed after a long day of predictions he may have taken the bus home to a small semi in the suburbs.

Nevertheless, mysterious and elusive, he became a key figure at Apple. In fact, such was his status during the first months of the organization that there were times when hugely important business decisions would be determined not by reasoned arguments thrashed out during board meetings but on the strength of Caleb's predictions. And a number of key posts and positions within Apple were determined in a similar way. This sounds pretty unbelievable, I know. If it's any consolation, it was pretty unbelievable at the time, although within the context of Apple's eccentric universe it seemed infinitely more normal then than in retrospect. John once famously likened Apple's business ventures to playing Monopoly with real money. Whenever I think of that quote I remember Caleb sitting cross-legged on the floor with a look of concentration on his face throwing the I-Ching.

Mal Evans was another key figure at Apple. Originally a bouncer at Liverpool's Cavern Club, he was hired by Brian in 1963 as a roadie for the Beatles. When Brian died and Apple was founded, Mal had continued as the group's personal assistant. A huge, gentle bear of a man, he had a vulnerable charm and, like Neil, a dedication to the Beatles which went way beyond mere servitude. In a way he was more of a companion to them, someone whose long-standing relationship with them resulted in mutual trust and understanding.

Mal was a tremendously warm and humorous person and, again like Neil, had an almost telepathic understanding of the Beatles' day-to-day requirements. They could not have had a better assistant. He always seemed able to get hold of anything they needed and was always in the right place at the right time. Because most of his working life was dedicated to the group, their eventual split hit him very hard. Bored and directionless, he moved to Los Angeles in the early seventies where he began work on a book of memoirs entitled *Living the Beatles Legend*. He also became involved with drugs. Shortly before the book was completed in 1976 he overdosed on valium and grabbed an unloaded shotgun which he started waving around. The police were called and when they arrived Mal pointed the gun at them. Taking no chances, they shot him dead. His premature death, at the age of forty, was a genuine tragedy. His ashes were sent back to the UK, but they were lost in the post, prompting John Lennon's remark that poor Mal had ended up in 'the dead letter office'!

One of my favourite characters at Apple was press officer Derek Taylor. Having already worked for the Beatles in Brian's era (in fact he ghosted his autobiography *A Cellar Full of Noise*), the band turned to him when they formed Apple, and he moved back from the USA to join the organization. I liked him enormously, and he understood the Beatles as well as anyone did. He had an immense love of films, so we had a great mutual interest. He was also a supremely talented press officer, capable of writing excellent copy to tight deadlines. He was incredibly personable in his own eccentric way, addressing everyone as 'squire' or 'vicar'. I can't remember which I was! Despite – perhaps because of – his considerable appetite for drink and drugs, he had a great flair for flamboyantly entertaining the press and other visitors to the Apple offices. I was saddened to hear of his recent death. Although I hadn't seen him for several years, I remember him as a true individual and a likeable man whose wit and bonhomie will be sorely missed.

On our return from India it was decided that the Apple organization should have some kind of official launch in the USA. Somebody – I suspect it was Derek – came up with the idea of arranging a series of press conferences, chat-show appearances and other publicity-related events. So we did just that, and John and Paul, Neil, Brian Lewis, Magic Alex, Derek, Mal and I flew out to New York on 11 May.

Like the rest of us, John and Paul were going to stay at the luxurious St Regis Hotel, where a series of press interviews were scheduled. However, when we arrived, the place was besieged by hordes of fans, and it was subsequently arranged that the group move into the apartment of their friend the lawyer Nat Weiss who lived close by, while the rest of us stayed at the St Regis. This was a poignant reminder of just how confined the boys' lives had become, particularly after the freedom of India. In fact Mal later told me that it had become virtually impossible for any member of the group to book a hotel without the rooms being infiltrated by obsessive female fans and groupies whom he would be deployed to remove. How they got there was a mystery. I suspect a combination of bribery and/or forced entry were the usual methods. This seems rather surprising, but to Mal and Neil, who had accompanied them throughout their touring days, it was routine.

Life at the hotel was pretty confined for the Apple entourage, and we had to make our own fun. I've never really been into smoking dope, but I remember that one night Paul visited the suite that Neil and I were sharing and we got so stoned on pot that we spent several hours decorating an enormous plant in the communal suite with letters, business cards and hotel writing paper.

It was agreed that the first official Apple 'board meeting', as it was billed, should take place somewhere unusual. So on 12 May we spent the day in meetings on a Chinese junk that sailed around the Statue of Liberty. This particular stunt was probably thought up by Derek. At any rate, he entered the spirit of the proceedings with gusto, even donning a sailor's cap. We didn't do much at the inaugural meeting. We took a few photographs on the boat and we had a bit of a chat while circumnavigating the statue. Nothing, at least as I remember it, was discussed of any significance. The following day was spent giving press interviews at the St Regis, and then on Tuesday 14 May a major press conference was conducted at the Americana Hotel.

Despite his confinement at the hotel and at Nat's apartment Paul managed once or twice to meet up with Linda Eastman, a talented photographer with whom a romance was beginning to blossom. They hooked up at the press conference, at which Linda took pictures, and she later accompanied Paul to the airport on his return to London. Their relationship would subsequently intensify over the year, with meetings and visits in Los Angeles, London and New York. On many of these occasions Paul and Linda managed to retain their privacy, despite the fact that they would often walk freely on the streets of these cities. This was possible largely because throughout 1968 Paul had become a master of disguise. He greatly valued being able to do the things that most of us take for granted, such as taking a bus or walking in a park, and was not prepared to let his celebrity status prevent him from doing normal, everyday things. In an effort to retain his anonymity he had learned to dress and behave in a manner that would prevent him from being recognized. He managed to achieve this by wearing very ordinary clothes that seemed to come from a previous era. In fact some of them did. During that year he bought a great many garments secondhand from Portobello Market and frequently travelled to the Wigmore Street offices by bus. When I questioned him about his unconventional fashion sense, he replied, 'Denis, you have to understand, these are clothes that you can move about in.' Whether he was referring to the cut of the cloth or the anonymity they afforded him I am not sure; perhaps both. If you have studied the Beatles' lyrics you will know that they were masters of the double meaning!

Cynics may interpret this as another example of Paul's supposed meanness. They are entirely wrong. It is a manifestation of one of his most endearing character traits, a love of the ordinary and a desire to exist in the same world as the rest of us. He desperately wants to retain a sense of his roots and keep his feet on the ground in order to counterbalance the unreality and artificiality of celebrity. This ambition served him well while he was a Beatle and has continued to do so ever since. Celebrity can be the most destructive invention of the modern world, and Paul knows this all too well.

Although we had come to the USA to launch Apple publicly, the interviewers and journalists at the Americana had a different agenda. They seemed more interested in the Beatles' dealings with the Maharishi than anything else, and John and Paul constantly had to deflect attention on to the subject that we had come across the Atlantic to promote. Later that evening things got even worse when John and Paul arranged to publicize Apple on Johnny Carson's *Tonight Show* on NBC. It would be inaccurate to say that the interview was a complete disaster for the two Beatles. They were their usual amiable selves and at least managed to announce the formation of Apple and their plans to patronize young artists to millions of viewers. But the show could not have been handled more amateurishly by its producers.

To begin with, there was such a demand for places in the audience that major celebrities who wanted to attend could not get in. Paul Simon and Art Garfunkel were just two. According to one source, they were promised tickets, but when they turned up at the studios found that their reserved seats were already occupied by two impersonators! Superstar crooner Tony Bennett, who had brought his Beatles-obsessed son to watch the show, managed, with my help, to get autographs, but a post-show meeting proved impossible to arrange. Security around John and Paul was so tight before and after the programme that he couldn't get near them. And when the show began, the Beatles were interviewed not by Carson, a seasoned and articulate professional, but by Joe Garagiola, a great baseball player but not the world's greatest chat-show host. His frequently inane questions led to an awkward interview – not aided by the presence of actress Tallulah Bankhead, who, seemingly inebriated, savaged most attempts at serious discussion with a series of interruptions which gave Joe's banal questions a good run for their money. As far as I was concerned, the

115

trip was something of a non-event, even if it achieved its objective of publicizing the new company.

When we returned to London we found ourselves swamped by a wave of incoming mail from would-be writers, musicians, songwriters and film-makers in the USA. The American launch ultimately produced nothing in the way of new discoveries. Like Paul's adverts and bill posters, we merely ended up encouraging an enormous pile of uninteresting and unreadable drivel. Our efforts to sift through this useless material also proved expensive. I can't speak for Apple Records, but the film department was at one point forced to employ five full-time readers to wade through the flood of submissions that arrived day after day. Everybody, it seemed, wanted a bite of the Apple.

In retrospect, I suppose that we should have been prepared for the consequences of what we were doing by inviting the public to send us their material. We should have known that it would inspire a mass of responses that we were simply incapable of dealing with. In a way the episode says a great deal about Apple's first incarnation, of its well-intentioned idealism and of the disorganization that would gradually bring it to its knees.

Although it became obvious that wading through the slush pile wasn't going to produce a viable or interesting new film project, my determination to get a new Beatles movie or television show off the ground was as strong as ever. And if I couldn't find a specific script, what the hell? I could at least put the framework of new ideas together and push them as far as development stage.

One of the reasons why the Beatles' film projects kept falling through, I reasoned, was that the group found the process of film-making boring. They loved films and, with the exception of *Help!*, were proud of much of what they had achieved cinematically. However, the stumbling block was the prospect of having to commit themselves to a long-term project that would tie them up for months on end. Following the prolonged editing period of *Magical Mystery Tour*, the Beatles were now all too aware of how long films take to put together. I think it is also possible that they were still smarting from the critical pasting they had received. There is no doubt that they had had their fingers badly burned.

Several projects had already been mooted by Apple Films, although none were intended for the Beatles. One such film was *Walkabout*, a highly original story of the relationship between a young adolescent girl, her younger brother and an aboriginal boy who helps them to survive when they get lost in the hostile Australian outback. Knowing that it had excellent cinematic potential, I had acquired the film rights of the book early in 1967, just before the formation of Apple. I felt that it would make an ideal first picture for Nic Roeg as director/photographer. However, following his work on *Petulia*, Nic became involved in co-directing *Performance* with Donald Cammell, so the project was put on the back-burner. He was, however, captivated by the subject matter and knew that it would lend itself perfectly to his visionary style. I considered the possibility of doing the film (with Nic directing) through Apple Films. Unfortunately the film division was not particularly flush, and its in-house funds were not sufficient to cover the cost of a major feature. If this sounds strange, remember that the film department was just one part of the burgeoning Apple empire and had only around £40,000 at its disposal at any one time. That wouldn't have stopped us from raising finance from a major distributor such as United Artists or Warner Brothers, both of whom were highly active in Britain at the time. However, when these funds didn't materialize I gave my option on the book to Nic, who desperately wanted to direct the film version and literally begged me for the rights. The film subsequently became a great success and a landmark for its director, who captured perfectly the eerie beauty of the outback in one of the most poetically realized literary adaptations of the decade. It's just a pity that it wasn't an Apple film.

With *The Lord of the Rings* I had come close to getting a major project starring the Beatles off the ground. That idea had been well developed when finally it fell through. But, although it was the first time, it certainly would not be the last that I would conceive a project, get the Beatles' enthusiastic involvement, interest a director in it, even raise the finance, only to see my hopes dashed at the last minute. There were several others that occurred during and around the first four or five months of 1968.

The unwitting genesis of the first of these abandoned projects occurred almost twenty years earlier in 1949. During that year I had worked as assistant director on a period melodrama called *Trottie True*, the story of a Gaiety Girl who marries a lord. The film, directed by Brian Desmond Hurst and starring Jean Kent, had been shot partially on location at the beautiful and elegant setting of the Edwardian gardens at Stowe Public School in Buckinghamshire. There is a scene in which the Edwardian impresario, George Edwardes, takes his girls on a picnic in the grounds. Remembering the splendour of the setting and surrounding architecture, it occurred to me that this could be an excellent place for the Beatles to play for a live television performance.

Given the pronounced Edwardian bent of English psychedelic fashions, I thought the imposing gardens and buildings would lend a suitable period ambience to a concert featuring the band and envisaged the production as a kind of filmic rendition of the *Sergeant Pepper* cover. Like millions of others I had been enchanted by Peter Blake's arresting cover image. The performance special was inspired partly by the spirit of the cover, the idea of a good-natured psychedelic 'happening' played out in Edwardian finery and surroundings, with the Beatles supported by a variety of their friends and contemporaries, possibly including the Rolling Stones and Donovan.

By pure coincidence the group had already played inside the school some five years earlier, as I later found out. In April 1963 Brian had accepted a £100 booking from the school to perform an exclusive show for an audience of public schoolboys. More used to playing to the screaming teenage girls of the Cavern or the strippers and bruisers of Hamburg, it must have felt pretty strange for the Beatles to play to such a well-behaved and privileged audience. According to the reports and pictures I have seen, no dancing, cheering or any other kind of spontaneous display of enjoyment was allowed by the schoolmasters. The boys simply showed their appreciation by clapping politely after each number.

I discussed the Stowe project with British director Ken Russell, who had recently made an extraordinary impact on television audiences with his direction of a series of highly subjective and flamboyant portraits of classical composers. He was very keen to get involved. However, although the Beatles were enthusiastic about the project for a while, they ultimately lost interest and plans were scrapped. Later the same year the Rolling Stones made their infamous *Rock and Roll Circus* film (featuring a blistering performance of 'Yer Blues' by John), which followed a similar period variety-show approach. Our film never got made, but the Stones' film didn't get released – at least not until many years later in 1995. They were, according to rumours circulating at the time, unhappy with their performance.

The most memorable of the aborted projects was a film that paired the Beatles with maverick French film director Jean-Luc Godard. I had long been an admirer of Godard's experimental and challenging direction, and on the strength of commercial and critical successes such as *A Bout de Souffle* (1959), *Le Mépris* (1963), *Alphaville* (1965) and *Weekend* (1967) felt sure that the marriage would easily find backing from a distributor. I also knew that Godard liked to shoot his material fairly quickly and figured that he would therefore be perfect for the Beatles. After some brief conversations with the group, I contacted Godard proposing that we meet to discuss the project, which we did. When he came to the Apple offices he was the complete antithesis of his public persona. I found the *enfant terrible* of the cinema a charming, softly spoken and polite man, quite the opposite of many directors I can think of. But what would we film? My suggestion was that he make a kind of 'Day in the Life' documentary of the group in his own inimitable style, a kind of perverse, counter-cinema version of *A Hard Day's Night*. I also suggested a title *One Plus One* which, although meaningless, had a ring to it that captured my imagination. I thought it would make a good movie title. However, no specific subject matter was broached and it was decided that Godard would develop some ideas of his own. It was also agreed that he would shoot whatever he needed within a three-week time-span.

Finding a distributor wasn't difficult, despite the vagueness of the project. The teaming of the world's most famous band with a filmmaker of Godard's renown was enough. I merely called Bud Ornstein, by now head of European production at Paramount, and discussed things with him. An outline contract was drawn up and the Beatles were set, at least provisionally, to appear in their next film.

Then one Sunday shortly afterwards I was enjoying a leisurely afternoon at my house in St George's Square when I received a telephone call from Paul.

'Denis, I need to talk to you about something. Can I come over to see you?'

'Of course. When?'

'Now.'

I suggested that he join us for tea. He happily accepted the invitation and said he'd be there in an hour.

Paul's tone had been light-hearted, but I knew that this had to be something pretty serious. The Beatles tended not to keep the same hours as the rest of the world, so this was highly unusual. He arrived around four and we exchanged family news over tea.

Eventually we got round to what was on Paul's mind. George did not want to make the film, and since the Beatles never did anything unless all four were in agreement the Godard movie could not go ahead.

This was not good. Apart from my own personal financial disappointment at the decision, I genuinely believed that the Beatles and Godard would have worked together well. More important was the fact that the group had a contract with Paramount they had to honour. I explained to Paul that if they decided to drop the film they could be sued by Paramount for breach of contract, but he was adamant that the group would not participate in the movie.

'But what about this, Paul?' I asked, waving a copy of the contract at him.

'Give it to me,' he said, grinning. 'I'll drop it in the Thames on the way home.'

I was momentarily speechless. He took the contract, smiled and, thanking us for the tea, sauntered out.

This, I thought to myself, is simply not happening. If we terminate the contract Paramount could take us to the cleaners. In the film industry contracts are taken extremely seriously. You certainly don't just chuck them in the river the minute they don't suit you! But the Beatles had scant regard for contracts and other niceties. This was perhaps a hangover from their days with Brian. Under his management they had most of this kind of thing taken care of by him, and they had little to do with contractual details, rarely concerning themselves with what they regarded as legal minutiae. Even their dealings with Brian himself were rarely cemented by official documentation.

Fortunately I was on good terms with Bud. My solid relationship with him, combined with some skilful back-up from Brian Lewis, meant that I was able to resolve a problem that could otherwise have cost the Beatles dearly in breach-of-contract lawsuits. Shortly after this Godard went on to film the Stones for *One Plus One: Sympathy for the Devil*, which came out later that year. He evidently liked the title as much as I did.

Incidentally, I never found out whether Paul actually did dump the contract in the Thames that evening. I certainly hope so. One thing is certain. I don't ever want to see it again!

*

Elsewhere at Apple things weren't running particularly smoothly. Seven months after the Apple Boutique had opened the Beatles decided that it should be closed down. The whole thing had been a complete and unmitigated disaster. The initial idea, a hybrid combining 'swinging London' sensibilities with hippy philosophy and style, was that the shop would sell an outstanding mixture of groundbreaking products. It was envisaged as a 'beautiful place where you could buy beautiful things'. Unfortunately by summer 1968 and the waning of flower power The Fool's designs began to look increasingly like relics from another age and, despite its grand conception, the boutique looked and felt little different to any of the 'head' stores in London at the time. Its one outstanding feature, the remarkable psychedelic mural that The Fool had designed for the shop's exterior, had been removed as a result of complaints to the local authorities. Outdated and impractical, the Apple Boutique had not been the great triumph that the Beatles had hoped for.

There was a clear sense of inevitability in all this. The shop should never have opened in the first place or at least not the way that it did. In the rag trade it is common to take goods on a sale-or-return basis, but the Beatles took on The Fool for an enormous signing-on fee of some £40,000. As well as being unnecessary, this was a ludicrous figure in 1968. At one point we got the London School of Economics to analyse the logistics of the enterprise. It estimated that, on the figures we had given it, Apple would have to open a chain of at least nine stores even to begin to approach economic viability. When in July 1968 the boutique was closed down, thousands more were lost after it was decided to give away the stock to the public, many of whom queued for hours to receive their freebies.

The closing of the store heralded the end of the Beatles' association with The Fool. Shortly after they left Apple they recorded an LP for Mercury Records following a deal that reputedly involved an enormous advance and a legal stipulation that the executives would not be permitted to hear any work in progress.[1] I shudder to think what went through their heads when they were privileged finally to hear the results of their expensive new signing. Only a handful of albums were actually sold, but its awful, affected, self-regarding grandeur remains a poignant reminder to aficionados of sixties pop that by no means everything from that era warrants another listen. In the words of the Tremeloes, sometimes silence is golden.

8

Another Day at the Office

THIRTY YEARS AFTER the Beatles' split I am still responding to a steady stream of questions about the group by friends and fans. I thought that the interest in the group would eventually wane, but, if anything, it has grown. The fascination that the Beatles generate is, it seems, destined to continue for ever. Many of the queries I receive are so general or banal that they are virtually impossible to answer. Here, together with my usual responses, are some of the most common.

Question: 'Who was the most talented Beatle?'

Rather weary reply: 'All of them. They were all incredibly talented in their own ways.'

Question: 'Which one did you like the most?'

Weary reply: 'I liked them all very much, in different ways.'

Question: 'What were they like?'

Weary reply: 'They were great.'

Question: 'Yes, but what about John. What was he like?'

Very weary reply: 'He was a great guy.'

Question: 'And Paul? What was he like?'

Very, very weary reply: 'He was great, too.'

Question: 'What about Ringo?'

I've usually dropped off to sleep by this point. (For the record, both Ringo and George were 'great', too.)

I say this not to criticize those earnest fans who are genuinely intrigued by what was, after all, a fascinating phenomenon. I simply mention it to illustrate the fact that one is most often asked questions

125

that are fundamentally unanswerable. I suppose I should take a lesson from the Beatles and come up with witty or cutting responses, but I would rather avoid offending the fans and keep my friends.

I was recently asked one question, however, that I don't think I had ever been asked before. It was a simple one, but it made me stop and think. It was: 'Can you describe a typical day at Apple?' My immediate response was: 'No, there was always something different happening', and in a way that is God's honest truth. But in a way the 'typical' or 'ordinary' was paradoxically the untypical, the extraordinary or the just plain fantastic. There was no typical, ordinary day working for the Beatles at Apple, but, for what it's worth, here's a recollection of a day in 1968 that summarizes the 'ordinary' extraordinariness of it all, one that demonstrates all the hassle, frustrations, happiness and exhilaration rolled into the space of less than twenty-four hours.

One summer morning, shortly before Apple relocated to its Savile Row offices, I was wading through a pile of scripts when Paul walked into my office.

'Denis, we're going to a wedding this morning.'

'Oh,' I responded nonchalantly. 'Anyone I know?'

'Yeah, Magic Alex.'

'Very nice.'

'The only thing is,' Paul continued, 'we've got to sort out a wedding party for him.'

'When for?'

'Today. Straight after the service. For about fifty people.'

My heart sank, knowing that the 'we' in Paul's plans really meant me. 'You must be joking,' I said. 'We'll never sort out anything at this short notice.' I explained to him that you cannot organize a dinner for fifty guests ten minutes before you want to arrive; it simply wasn't a realistic request.

'See what you can do,' he said and made his exit.

This was typical of them. They had no real perspective on the planning that was needed to arrange something like this. This attitude was not born out of arrogance and, as I've mentioned, Paul in particular made a concerted effort to lead as normal a life as possible under the circumstances. Rather, it was a product of celebrity conditioning. They were simply out of touch with the workings of the real world and were not used to organizing anything for themselves. They just assumed that you could say the magic word 'Beatles' and any doors would simply be charmed open. However, Paul was, as I was about to find out, absolutely right.

The only place I could think of where I felt I might be able to pull any sort of rank was the exclusive Arethusa Club, which I had frequented many times and which was an occasional haunt of the Beatles. I phoned them without much hope, asked for the manager and relayed my request, making no reference to the Fab Four. I suppose I wanted to see how far I could get without resorting to celebrity name-dropping or grovelling, two things I have always hated.

'I'm very sorry, sir,' the Arethusa's manager told me evenly, although he obviously thought I was barking mad or had been living in a mud hut for the past ten years. 'These things have to be booked months in advance.'

'Is there nothing you can do?' I implored, with all the desperation I could muster.

'Absolutely not,' came the predictable and rather smug reply. 'We're completely, totally, fully booked.'

There are times when you simply have to put any principles of fairness and decency to one side and blatantly exploit the few genuine privileges celebrity brings. 'There will be some very important guests,' I continued, moving in for the kill.

'Oh yes?' was the rather non-committal response. He had obviously heard this sort of thing a thousand times before.

'It's for the Beatles,' I told him, stooping to conquer.

There was a brief pause while the word worked its magic and the manager's personality was transformed from detached jobsworth to flattering toady of the first division.

'One moment please, sir,' he gushed. Another brief silence was followed by some distant muttering in the background. 'We would be most happy indeed to fit you in for lunch this afternoon.'

'That's very kind,' I replied, barely bothering to conceal my own insincerity.

Paul and the other Beatles were delighted with the news and, after Alex's Greek Orthodox wedding, at which John was best man, a superb party was had by all. After the celebrations Paul and I drove back to Apple's offices and drank whisky and coke.

'Come and listen to this, Denis,' he said, ushering me into a side office. Setting up a tape recorder in the room, he played me a demo of a new song that he had just recorded. It was a long, powerful track, beautifully structured with an irresistible sing-along refrain, perhaps the prototype of what DJs now refer to as a 'power ballad'. It had a melody to die for, with a melancholic quality that was somehow simultaneously uplifting. Desperate yet assured, forlorn yet optimistic, the song had an emotional resonance that went far beyond anything I'd heard before on a pop record. It had a magic that only a Beatle could conjure. I felt then, and still feel today, that 'Hey Jude' was the apotheosis, the pinnacle of Paul's songwriting as a Beatle and one of the most glorious pieces of music of the past century.

As the song came to a close, Paul's voice brought me back down to earth. 'Do you think it could be a single?' he asked. Although not finished, the song was pretty long and he was concerned that EMI would reject it on these grounds.

'It's a wonderful song, Paul. I'm sure they'll make an exception.'

And that, believe it or not, was just another day at the office!

'Hey Jude'/'Revolution' was the first single by the group to be released on Apple Records and required promo clips to market it internationally. As head of Apple Films it was down to me to produce the clip. We never had any serious discussions on how to film the promos, but a couple of days before the shoot an instruction from Paul appeared on my desk. It was vague and non-constructive. I felt that since the A-side was essentially a sing-along this should be echoed visually in the promo clip, with a studio audience joining in live for the final extended refrain.

The problem, however, was that the Beatles didn't want to have anything to do with a conventional live performance. By 1968 they were genuinely terrified of playing in front of an audience and had refused to undertake any live work for two years. Although their last concert performance had taken place at Candlestick Park in San Francisco, the turning-point had come the month before, after a particularly bad experience in the Philippines. Following a misunderstanding with the palace in Manila, the Beatles were hounded out of the country after failing to appear at a dinner hosted by President Ferdinand Marcos and his wife Imelda, and their terrifying exit from the country had been the final straw. Aside from the ever-present concerns over security, playing live had also become pointless artistically anyway, since most of their recordings after *Rubber Soul* involved far more than a four-piece ensemble. Looking back, it is genuinely surprising that they remained a live band for as long as they did, although of course the Beatles' decision to become entirely a 'studio band' was itself unprecedented at the time.

That did not change the fact that I envisaged 'Hey Jude' as a song that would lend itself visually to some kind of live concert footage. After serious consideration I hit on the idea of arranging the shoot at Twickenham Studios with the group performing to an invited audience. Michael Lindsay-Hogg was hired to direct the filming. To be honest, I had never been a particular fan of his work, but I reasoned that he was familiar with the form (he had already directed the 'Paperback Writer'/'Rain' clips back in 1966) and was not the kind of director whose presence would invite clashes of ego.[1]

My assistant, Tony Bramwell, was dispatched to invite an impromptu audience of fans literally from off the streets and to transport them in three or four coaches to the studio for the shoot. Leaflets were also handed out around Twickenham, and Mal rounded up a crowd of 'Apple scruffs' from outside the recently acquired Savile Row offices. Tony did a great job, and we ended up with a terrific range of ages and nationalities. With some trepidation we began shooting late in the afternoon, with David Frost taping an intro that would make the performance appear as if it had been specially arranged as part of London Weekend Television's *Frost on Sunday* show. As a further precaution to ease the Beatles' acute anxiety about being mobbed, I placed them on rostrums to keep them at arm's length from the audience. As it turned out I needn't have worried, and as the group's anxiety abated they became less and less self-conscious, finally allowing the audience on to the rostrum with them for the final sing-along. My young son Kevan made it into the final cut of the video, smiling from behind Ringo's drum kit. The intention was that we should finish filming early that evening. As it happened, everyone was having so much fun that the filming went on into the early hours of the next day.

'Hey Jude' became the Beatles' biggest-selling single and was included in the *Our First Four* promotional box sets put together by Apple Records. Comprising the Beatles' 'Hey Jude', Mary Hopkin's 'Those Were the Days', the Black Dyke Mill's Band's 'Thingumybob' (both produced by Paul) and the George Harrison-produced Jackie Lomax track 'Sour Milk Sea', the collection made an impressive package. For publicity purposes we sent copies to 10 Downing Street and Buckingham Palace. I'm not sure what the Queen made of it all![2]

The 'Hey Jude' promo is possibly more important than most fans realize. The Beatles' unexpected enjoyment at performing for the clip was to be a key factor in the new direction that they were about to take. After shooting we ran the final edit of the tapes in the recording truck. They were absolutely delighted. Drinking a whisky and coke with them at four in the morning, we agreed that a good night had been had by all. In fact they had enjoyed it so much they suggested, there and then, that we should make another film. I was elated. That was the start of *Let It Be*.

PART 3
Apple Crumble

Unhappy New Year

OFFICIAL VERSIONS OF the Beatles' history will tell you that the group split over the bitter feud about the control of their business interests, and there is no question that, at least to a degree, this is true. But artistically the seeds of the group's creative disharmony were sown during the making of the 'White Album'. The recording sessions had certainly been difficult at times, despite the unquestionably glorious finished work.

The musical visions and styles of the group were becoming more and more disparate. Paul had become increasingly intent on honing his extraordinary pastiche sensibilities, this time assimilating influences from Jamaican rhythms ('Ob-la-di, Ob-la-da'), music hall or vaudeville ('Honey Pie'), country and western ('Rocky Racoon') and even surf music in his brilliant Beach Boys parody 'Back in the USSR'. John's compositions were equally beguiling in their stylistic breadth, including the avant-garde sound collage 'Revolution 9', the charming lullaby 'Goodnight', folk songs such as 'Julia' and the explosive, visceral rock of 'Yer Blues'. George, too, had been busy composing, with songs such as 'While My Guitar Gently Weeps' and 'Long Long Long' showcasing his songwriting talents and establishing him as a gifted and sensitive composer. In fact, by now he was unquestionably capable of producing original pieces that were equal in stature to much of Lennon and McCartney's output.[1]

Although the artistic acrimony that existed at the time has been exaggerated, there is no doubt that the Beatles were developing diverse musical interests and that these were the source of some tension. And while they created a rich tapestry of musical textures for the album this undoubtedly contributed to the fragmentation of their musical relationships, as is evinced by the conspicuously small number of tracks that featured all four musicians playing together. Some, such as Paul's 'Blackbird' and John's 'Julia', were effectively solo works. Although John and Paul had not always composed together, they had certainly collaborated frequently with one other. By the release of the 'White Album', however, it was becoming increasingly clear that the collaborative aspect of their partnership was beginning to dissolve.

In fact, if John was working with anybody regularly now it was with the Japanese conceptual artist Yoko Ono, who became his partner after the break-up with his wife Cynthia.

There is no doubt at all that while Yoko was good for John she could be seen as invasive and demanding, even before she and John became lovers in May 1968, just before the group began recording the 'White Album'. They had famously first met at one of her Indica Gallery exhibitions in London during November 1966, where they struck up an instant rapport. Although it would be some eighteen months before the relationship was consummated, Yoko spent a great deal of time at Apple in the early months of 1968 simultaneously trying to woo John and to hustle various members of the company for financial backing for her projects. By this point she had already achieved minor notoriety. This stemmed predominantly from her then shocking avant-garde film *Bottoms*, a short consisting of nude close-ups of men's and women's buttocks. The great and the good, the rich and the poor, the fat and the thin: Yoko's controversial film did not discriminate. I rather admired her cheek. Despite her diminutive stature Yoko was an extraordinarily formidable and intelligent woman, and, as John fell slowly but surely under her spell, her presence at the Apple headquarters had become ever stronger. The Beatles' main office even became home to one of Yoko's conceptual pieces, a gradually rotting green apple placed on a pedestal. It had, by sheer coincidence, been created before the establishment of the company, but it was an ominous warning. There were times when she even became a piece of conceptual art herself, hanging out in our offices in a black bag. An odd way to make friends and do business, but it obviously worked – for her at least.

One of her earliest Beatles-related projects was another conceptual piece, and she had approached me at Apple Films for finance. She wanted £10,000 for a film that was provisionally – and rather provocatively – entitled *One Thousand Ways*. Ten thousand pounds sounded like a reasonable amount to ask for what I assumed would be a highly profitable avant-garde porn movie, but I lost interest when I discovered the 'one thousand ways' of the title referred to different birthing methods. I refused, on the grounds that stock footage of this kind already existed in hospitals and other medical institutions. I was all for experimentation, but I couldn't understand why she couldn't use existing footage.

Because of her relationship with John the other Beatles and Apple staff tolerated Yoko's presence, although the group's patience was severely tested when it came to making records. Much to the chagrin of the other members of the Beatles, Yoko was present throughout much of the recording of the 'White Album'. Indeed John's most collaborative work on the LP is 'Revolution 9', which proved to be the first of several such pieces released by John and Yoko during the late sixties. Paul hated it and unsuccessfully did his best to keep it off the album, while the fans earnestly tried to understand what it was all about.

The fraught atmosphere came to a head when Ringo left the group for two weeks.[2] He felt – wrongly – that his playing had declined, and he may have been alienated by the increasingly individualized nature of the project. Although the 'White Album' became one of the world's fastest-selling LPs, its production was anything but happy.

Production of the 'White Album' was a relatively straightforward affair, however, by comparison with their next project. How does one begin to discuss *Let It Be*? The subtitle of a recent book about it, Sulphy and

135

Schweighardt's *Get Back*, labelled the whole thing a disaster, and I suppose in some respects it was, albeit, at times, a glorious one.

The Beatles had greatly enjoyed making the 'Hey Jude' and 'Revolution' promos we did that September at Twickenham, and it was from them that many of the ideas for what eventually turned into the *Let It Be* movie developed in late 1968. They felt that filming those clips had been a great experience after some of the unhappy tours they had undertaken and that it had been wonderful to play in front of a 'controlled' live audience. The initial concept of *Let It Be* (or *Get Back*, as it was first known) was that the group would perform a concert in front of an audience which would be filmed and released both as a TV special and an album. The project was really Paul's baby. By this point he had become the key instigator of many of the Beatles' activities, and it was he who took control of the project. He felt that it was high time the Beatles regrouped to get back to their rock-and-roll roots and to make music that was apparently untouched by studio trickery.

I thought, in principle, that it was a terrific idea. In view of the somewhat fraught atmosphere that had pervaded the recording of the 'White Album' I felt that playing live as a four-piece ensemble would help to restore the group's unity and reaffirm what had brought them together in the first place. In the process, they would revisit British skiffle and American rock and roll, the fifties popular musical styles that had first united them; I hoped that their mutual love of their musical heritage might keep them together at a time of increasingly heated business and artistic disagreements.

The original plan was that the footage would simply be a concert special that didn't include anything else in the way of extra material. The way I envisaged it, the structure of the final product should echo the minimalism of the Beatles' new approach; it should be earthy, basic and simple. I reasoned that seeing the Beatles playing together live once more would be enough for audiences. No frills, just the Beatles performing together for the first time since their swansong concert in San Francisco's Candlestick Park in August 1966.

The main dilemma was: 'Where do you stage a concert featuring the world's biggest band?' All of us thought it would be rather dull and old hat for them to stage another huge stadium-style event such as Shea or the Hollywood Bowl, so Neil, the group and myself tossed around a number of ideas for locations.

Many ideas were considered. One of my suggestions was that the group should play at a disused flour mill by the Thames. I had discovered this place years earlier while looking for film locations and felt that its eerie white emptiness might provide a good backdrop for the performance. I took John and Paul to see it but after briefly enthusing about its potential they decided that it wasn't quite what they had in mind. Another idea I had was for the group to play on the Cunard cruise liner the *Queen Elizabeth*, but its owners would not give us permission to cordon off a section of the ship, and in the end the Beatles decided that it wouldn't be practical. As more and more ideas were tossed about, a clear pattern began to emerge. The boys were only ever in agreement about a location for a day or so at most, making any negotiations with them – or with anyone else – virtually impossible.

My best idea, I thought, was for the group to play at a Roman amphitheatre in Zabratha, Tripoli, in North Africa. Many years earlier, after working on a film called *Sea of Sand*, I had been in Libya and seen a wonderful performance of Euripides' drama *Orestes* there, staged by the company of the Italian actor/producer Vittorio Gassman. I felt that the amphitheatre would make an ideal stage. It was right by the sea and had the most wonderful acoustics for an open-air venue. You could stand on the stage and talk, and the sound would carry right back into the audience. I thought it would be great for the Beatles to perform there for a local crowd. John was thrilled; he thought it was a fantastic idea, one that would provide a stunning visual backdrop to the concert. Paul was also keen for a while, although Ringo and George demonstrated less enthusiasm.

The situation was becoming intolerable, and it seemed that no decision about the location would ever be reached. Towards the end of

1968 the suggestions and discussions simply dried up. Sad and frustrating though this was, my energies were now largely directed elsewhere. I was deeply involved in the pre-production of *The Magic Christian*, a satirical comedy in which Ringo was to star alongside comedy legend Peter Sellers. Throughout my time at Apple I had retained my own office space at Twickenham, and since that was where the film was to be shot it made sense for me to work from there. *The Magic Christian* was set to become a major production, and it seemed that the Beatles' concert special was never going to happen. With the exception of Ringo, whom I saw in connection with shooting *The Magic Christian*, I heard nothing from the group. Then, right at the end of the year, I received a telephone call from Paul.

'Denis, what are we doing about the show?' he asked.

This was a complete bolt from the blue since I had assumed that the project had been scrapped or at least put on the back-burner for a while.

I tried to be as accommodating as possible. I suggested that I could delay the shooting of *The Magic Christian* for a few weeks and let them use the sound stage at Twickenham for rehearsals. I could then bring in a film crew to document the action and we could build whatever sets we deemed necessary to make the footage more visually interesting. I felt that it would be a shame not to get as much material as we could on film. It could, I figured, perhaps be used for a television documentary to help bolster interest in the concert performance special if it ever actually happened. At this point there was still no consensus as to where the live concert would take place. However, after consulting with the group, it was decided that we would once more bring in Michael Lindsay-Hogg to direct. After all, he had done an excellent job on the 'Hey Jude'/'Revolution' promos, and the group was at ease in his presence. He brought in a minimal crew, and on 2 January 1969 shooting of the rehearsals began in earnest.

And so began one of the most well-intentioned disasters in music history, as the sessions would continuously break down in a tirade of bitter arguments, apathy and hopeless disillusionment. The early rehearsal sessions could have been the Beatles' artistic salvation. Instead, they proved to be anything but. Believe me, I know. I watched it happen.

As it turned out, just about everything that could go badly did. Tired and creatively exhausted after the recording of the 'White Album', the group had little new material to rehearse, which was in itself a source of tension. This, combined with the fact that they had not played as a live band for several years, caused no little trepidation, and a good deal of the early rehearsing comprised third-rate covers of the fifties rock-and-roll numbers they had enjoyed in their youth. Quite unbelievably, it seemed at times as if the band had somehow been robbed of their talent overnight. It was as if they had metamorphosed from being the greatest pop group of the twentieth century into a washed-up pub band that hadn't had a booking for months. It seemed, for much of the two weeks at Twickenham, as if they had simply lost their desire to play professionally. For the first and possibly only sustained period in their musical career the Beatles had lost their spirit. All of this was compounded by the fact that the group had agreed a schedule that involved rehearsing during the daytime, partly to accommodate the filming. This was always going to prove difficult when they were used to working at night and in the much more comfortable, familiar and private seclusion of the Abbey Road studios.

Worse still, the venue for the concert was still a bone of contention and a cause of frequent disruption, the group being unable to come to any sort of agreement about where it would take place. The locations already suggested continued to be discussed, along with a variety of other ideas that ranged from the Royal Albert Hall to London's National Gallery. Meanwhile I continued to push for the amphitheatre, but, by this time, it was virtually impossible to get all four of them to agree on anything.

In interviews Paul has often mentioned the strong sense of democracy that existed within the Beatles and the fact that projects were usually dropped unless everybody agreed on them.[3] Usually this worked greatly to their advantage. When decisions were finally made, everybody could enter each new project with enthusiasm and commitment because it would be something they all wanted to do. But this could also place tremendous stress on the people who worked with them. As a film producer I knew how difficult it could be on a picture to get those involved to see eye to eye, as they often have very different ideas about how a project should be developed. But nothing could have prepared me for the Beatles. Unlike traditional actors who are bound by contractual obligations, they answered to nothing and, with Brian gone, nobody. Normally film stars are contractually bound to turn up on time to work, regardless of how they feel about the project or each other. I, however, was endeavouring to produce footage in an impossibly undisciplined environment with a group of stars who were not, by then, on good terms with each other and who behaved exactly as they wished. If someone didn't feel like turning up to rehearsals on time – or, indeed, at all – that's what happened. Motivation and discipline were commodities that the group sorely lacked. Five years earlier such problems would never have occurred, but, paradoxically, the power afforded the Beatles by their immense success had helped to hasten their demise.

The inability to come to a decision over the concert venue made a difficult situation even worse and, with the exception of the ever-enthusiastic Paul, the Beatles now seemed to be in a kind of apathetic free fall, with no agreed goal to work towards. Communication – or the lack of it – was at the heart of the problem. Throughout my career as a producer I had seen many major creative disagreements; arguments between leading stars and actors, between stars and directors, directors and designers, designers and camera crews. I've even been involved in a few myself. Such clashes are usually resolved, often very quickly, to the mutual satisfaction of all concerned and mostly to the benefit of the film. In short, disagreements are frequently productive. But that wasn't the case with the Beatles. They would never thrash out their differences with each other (or anybody else for that matter) in any sort of constructive or reasonable way. Instead, they would simply stop communicating with one another. Nothing ever got resolved, and the awkward silences formed a breeding ground for hostility and resentment.

After a week and a half of half-hearted rehearsal sessions in an atmosphere fraught with tension and hostility, George walked out. I wasn't watching the rehearsals when it happened; I was in my production office when Paul came storming in to explain the situation. Although outwardly calm, he looked physically exhausted.

'That's it,' he said.

'What do you mean?' I enquired.

'That's it. We've split up. George has gone.'

'You mean he's left?'

'Yup. We had a fight and he walked out. He just said, "See you round the clubs."'

Severely troubling though Paul's announcement was, I would be lying if I said that it was a surprise. In fact, I'm sure that if George hadn't walked out that day John or Ringo would have done so before much longer. I don't think Paul would have left, partly because he was most committed to keeping the Beatles together and also because he had played a key role in thinking up the project. Yet while there can be no doubting that in retrospect the timing and location of the Twickenham sessions was poor, the real problems were a combination of creative, financial and personal differences which ran much deeper than superficial disputes about film locations or time schedules. To understand exactly what went wrong it is necessary to look at the situation from four very different perspectives.

By the time the Twickenham sessions took place John just wasn't interested in being a Beatle any more. If it hadn't been for Paul's eagerness to maintain some semblance of unity within the group it is possible that the 'White Album' would have been the Beatles' last LP. John went along with the 'Get Back' project, but he certainly played no part in its instigation or in instigating anything else the Beatles did from this point on.

If the Beatles had a leader in their early years, one could say it was John. He certainly came across as the dominant and most articulate member during that period, and between 1963 and 1965 he probably had the edge on Paul in terms of both quantity and quality of recorded output. An LP like *A Hard Day's Night*, for example, is, with notable exceptions, predominately a collection of Lennon songs. But from 1967 onwards more and more of the Beatles' most memorable LP tracks and singles are McCartney compositions. Indeed, while John was the dominant A-side composer of four successive UK singles in 1964–5 ('A Hard Day's Night', 'I Feel Fine', Ticket to Ride' and 'Help!'), Paul was on a huge creative roll during the later years. In fact, of the Beatles' six final singles releases from 1968 to 1970 no fewer than four of the A-sides were written by Paul, including the best-selling 'Hey Jude'.[4] Of the two remaining singles, one ('Something') was written by George. And if *A Hard Day's Night* can be said to be 'John's' LP, it would be reasonable to acknowledge that *Sergeant Pepper* is predominantly 'Paul's'. After all, if one disregards George's 'Within You, Without You' and the co-written Lennon and McCartney songs such as 'A Day in the Life' and 'With a Little Help from My Friends', one is left with a considerable seven-to-three imbalance in Paul's favour. (This is, of course, an extremely reductionist way of looking at Paul's and John's creative contribution to the band. However, it does demonstrate, albeit crudely, the shift in the balance of creative power that occurred between the two of them.)

So why did John Lennon relinquish his dominance of the Beatles? In the early days the band had meant more to him than anything in the world. In fact, until around 1967–8 he was obsessive about the group's fortunes. Now it was as much as anybody could do to get him to turn up to rehearsals. It is probably fair to say that his personal and creative attachment to the other Beatles had been replaced by his totally uncompromising relationship with Yoko. She was by then his main artistic collaborator, effectively cuckolding Paul. Indeed, the *Two Virgins* LP (released November 1968), with its notorious nude portrait of the two of them on the cover, was nothing if not a clear indication of John's desire to work with her and to embrace more avant-garde forms of self-expression.

The fact is, John was absolutely besotted by Yoko, to the point where they almost *became* one person. She was with him twenty-four hours a day, seven days a week. As far as John was concerned, everything, even the Beatles, took second place to her. While I was pleased that John had found personal happiness, the fervor and intensity of their infatuation was not a little daunting to those around them, and it was clear that this situation was not good for group relations. There is no question that Yoko's presence during filming rankled with Paul, George and Ringo. After all, prior to her arrival on the scene the Beatles had usually rehearsed and recorded in private and, although occasionally friends and colleagues would drop in to sessions, their presence was fairly low key and unobtrusive.[5] George Martin, a couple of engineers and Mal and Neil were the only regulars at Beatles recording sessions.

Although I do not subscribe to the notion that Yoko was responsible for breaking up the Beatles, it is undeniable that the frosty atmosphere of the Twickenham sessions was partly down to her unwillingness to take a lower profile and be a little more sensitive to the Beatles' working practices. It is probably fair to say that chipping in with musical suggestions to the most successful pop group in the world did not endear her to Paul, George or Ringo. Nevertheless I don't believe they felt any deep-rooted personal animosity towards her. They certainly were not racist or sexist, as some accounts would have you believe. I think they simply found her presence off-putting and her suggestions invasive and unwelcome. However, they grudgingly tolerated her at the sessions, as they were wary of airing their frustrations with John, feeling – rightly, I imagine – that any request for a discussion about this, however reasonable, would simply result in John quitting the band.

His lack of interest and commitment to the rehearsals was possibly exacerbated by personal problems. On 21 November 1968, the day before the release of the 'White Album', Yoko had a miscarriage at London's Queen Charlotte Hospital. John was deeply distressed by this, even recording the dying baby's heartbeat, which was included in John's and Yoko's second avant-garde collection, *Life with the Lions*, in May 1969. He also found himself having to face a court appearance on a drugs charge a few days later at Marylebone Magistrates' Court. Although minor in financial terms (he was fined £150), the police bust one month earlier had proved traumatic for John, who was very anxious that it would lead to Yoko's deportation. In an effort to protect her, he claimed that the small quantity of cannabis discovered at the flat in Montagu Square belonged entirely to him. Years later his drugs conviction was to be a major obstacle in his efforts to obtain a green card for US residency.

Although his fine was for the possession of soft drugs, John had been experimenting with heroin just before and during the Twickenham sessions. I wasn't aware of this at the time, and to the best of my knowledge neither were the other Beatles. The degree to which this affected his creativity after the 'White Album' is a moot point, but it is interesting that, for all the collaborative avant-garde projects he was evolving with Yoko, he brought precious little new material to the studio rehearsals, and the bulk of the finished LP's songs were predominantly McCartney compositions. John's most significant contributions were limited to the glorious 'Across the Universe' (written and recorded in 1968), 'One After 909' (originally recorded in 1963 but discarded and remade), the lame 'Dig a Pony' and throwaways such as 'Dig It'. Creatively, this was not John Lennon's finest hour.

George, meanwhile, was also clearly frustrated. Like Paul and Ringo he resented Yoko's presence at the rehearsals. Worse still, both

George and Paul were angry with John about comments that he had made to journalist Ray Coleman of *Disc and Music Echo* about the parlous state of Apple's finances, saying that if things didn't improve the Beatles would be broke within six months.

However, George's main source of frustration derived from the fact that his development as a songwriter was not sufficiently appreciated by the other Beatles, particularly Paul, who tended to dominate the sessions with his own songs and ideas. Having emerged from John's and Paul's shadow with some excellent contributions to the 'White Album', he was producing some wonderful material that the other Beatles still seemed largely uninterested in. Songs of the calibre of 'All Things Must Pass' and 'Hear Me Lord' were briefly tried and then rejected or discarded in the general atmosphere of torpor and disenchantment. And even when his songs were rehearsed, they were tackled with even less enthusiasm from John, who showed little inclination to do any serious work on the wonderful 'I Me Mine'. Many of George's rejected songs would later emerge on his first post-Beatle release, the spell-binding *All Things Must Pass*. Although John's *Plastic Ono Band* and Paul's *Band on the Run* are frequently hailed as the finest post-Beatle solo works, George's magnificent triple LP, released the following year, is arguably the most underrated item of the solo years, crammed full of astonishing melodies and beautifully realized arrangements.

In retrospect, it is totally understandable that George felt aggrieved. What accentuated his frustration and made the situation intolerable for him was the fact that he had just had a very enjoyable time producing Jackie Lomax's Apple LP *Is This What You Want?* and visiting Bob Dylan and the Band at Woodstock. His return to work as a Beatle, following the dour atmosphere that pervaded the 'White Album' sessions, was, in the light of these developments, premature to say the least.

Ringo was frustrated for different reasons. Always the most affable and easy-going of the Beatles, he had nevertheless become increasingly dissatisfied with the limitations of being 'just' the Beatles' drummer and was keen to prove his worth outside the band. By this point in their career John, George and Paul had all 'proved themselves' to greater or lesser degrees on solo projects, and Ringo was naturally keen to find some other platform to demonstrate his considerable talents. Although the 'White Album' had included his first solo composition (the country-inflected 'Don't Pass Me By'), songwriting was never going to be Ringo's strong point, and he was itching to find something else he enjoyed at which he could excel.

From the beginning it was clear that he was the most natural actor out of all the Beatles, and his lack of formal training was more than compensated for by his deadpan humour and natural screen presence. His excellent performance in *A Hard Day's Night* had led Richard Lester to give him the virtual lead role in *Help!*, and in 1968 he had taken a cameo role as a Mexican gardener in the star-studded film version of Terry Southern's novel *Candy*.

By January 1969 and the start of the 'Get Back' project, Ringo had accepted my offer to star alongside Peter Sellers in *The Magic Christian*. He was a huge fan – and a personal friend – of Peter's and was genuinely thrilled at the prospect of his first starring role, and I got the feeling that during the rehearsals his mind was often elsewhere. Encouraged by Paul, he tolerated rather than enjoyed the sessions, dutifully playing along with the others but rarely displaying the good-will and bonhomie that had previously been so infectious and abundant.

For his part, Paul wanted desperately to keep the Beatles together, which, under the circumstances, was a virtual impossibility. Given the shroud of gloom and apathy that hung over the proceedings, it was unsurprising that he sometimes appeared like a bossy general, trying against all odds to rally his troops. But regardless of how he appeared in the final film, the truth is that he was simply trying his best to keep alive some kind of work ethic and to encourage some sort of group dynamic and enthusiasm for the project. Throughout the time at

Twickenham when I was attempting to persuade the Beatles to decide on the location for the live show, it was always Paul who was most willing to engage in discussion.

In one respect, there is no little irony in this. Although it was Paul who maintained the most enthusiasm for the group's continued existence, it was clear that it was Paul who was the most productive writer. If anything, he seemed to have the least to lose if the Beatles split up and pursued solo careers. I suspect that this apparent contradiction was not the result of any kind of deep-rooted insecurity over his ability to develop artistically. Rather, he saw himself as the Beatles' public relations ambassador and was also perhaps the group's biggest fan. The end of the Beatles was an unbearable proposition, one that he could not bear to contemplate.

My advice to him when he came to my office with news of George's walk-out was to remain calm and sit things out. I figured that George would come back once he had had cooled down. As it turned out, I was right, and following a group meeting a few days later he grudgingly returned on condition that the live concert idea be dropped altogether and that the Beatles reconvene at the Apple studios to finish work on the songs for the new LP. I wasn't particularly worried by this. After all, the Beatles' plans changed dramatically from one day to the next, and in the meantime it was agreed that we would continue shooting at the Apple studios. The 'Get Back' project still had a long way to go, and there would be many twists and turns before it would finally reach its completion and release as *Let It Be*, but there is no doubt that it had been a pretty rotten start to 1969. I remember thinking that things could only get better. For the Beatles, however, they were about to get worse . . .

10

We Can't Work It Out

WITH THE TWICKENHAM rehearsals behind them, the Beatles moved into the studios they had asked Magic Alex to build for them in the basement of Apple's Savile Row premises. The idea, which I think came from Paul, was that it would be useful for the group to have their own private studios where they could both record and be on hand to deal with business matters. Magic Alex volunteered for the job, confident that he could build a studio that would make George Martin's set-up at Abbey Road seem antiquated. He even boasted to the Beatles that his super-advanced, space-age studio would have 72-track recording facilities. At that time Abbey Road had just eight! Traditionally when recording, drummers use wood and cloth dampers around their drums to cut out microphone leakage. This may obscure their view of fellow musicians. Alex claimed that he could manufacture a damper from an invisible sonic beam, enabling better visual, and thus musical, coordination between the band as they played. This innovation sounded too good to be true. And it was.

When the group finally tried to make use of the studio, it immediately became obvious that yet again their faith in Magic Alex had been hopelessly misplaced. The project was an unmitigated disaster, and the 'studio' – if that's what it could be called – was totally unusable. EMI engineer Geoff Emerick later recalled that Alex's mixing console (which bore a considerable similarity to the control panel of a B-52 bomber) was later sold for £5 as scrap to a secondhand electronics shop on the Edgware Road.[1] The place had to be stripped bare and,

149

with the help of the ever-reliable George Martin, who had always seen through Alex's overblown claims, mobile equipment was brought in from Abbey Road and rigged up in the basement. Fortunately some good progress was finally made once the new recording equipment had been fitted. Although from this point I was increasingly diverted by preparations for *The Magic Christian*, I got the distinct feeling that group relations had improved.

While the sessions at Apple weren't exactly fun, they did at least mark the beginning of a more productive week of rehearsal and recording, with work mainly centred on 'Don't Let Me Down', 'I've Got a Feeling', 'Get Back' and 'Dig a Pony'. It was also the point at which other new songs were introduced, Ringo's charming 'Octopus's Garden' being an example. There is a lovely sequence, which made it into the movie, that features Ringo playing the song to George on the piano and George helping to work out the chords as John joins in on drums. Although the Beatles did little work on the song during the rehearsal week, it was sufficiently appealing for them to rework it for *Abbey Road* later in the year. This week was of great significance to the group. I think it represented the point at which they realized that they had to pull their socks up as far as creating new music was concerned and either get on with it or call it a day. It would be misleading to say that the Apple basement sessions were first class either musically or in terms of group dynamics, but there was at least a marked improvement in the general atmosphere.

Part of this, I am sure, was due to the arrival of acclaimed session musician Billy Preston, whom George brought in to play keyboards. Billy had known the group for some time, having first befriended them at the Star Club, Hamburg, in their early years. He had been a backing musician for Little Richard, with whom the Beatles shared a billing for a two-week stint in 1962. Paying a call on his old friends while in London, Billy was persuaded by George to join them for the rehearsals and recordings. His presence had a hugely positive influence on the proceedings, from both a personal and a musical perspective. The previous year, when the Beatles were recording the 'White Album', George had introduced Eric Clapton to perform the guitar solo for 'While My Guitar Gently Weeps'. As well as gracing the LP with an exquisite solo, the involvement of an outside party, whom the other band members knew and respected, fostered a more agreeable atmosphere, and bringing in Billy Preston had exactly the same effect. As George later commented, people tend to be on their best behaviour when they are in the company of guests. Billy's presence, while not completely trans- forming the atmosphere, certainly helped reduce the petty bickering that had been such a feature at Twickenham. Indeed, he was a fine musician, and the presence of his keyboard-playing helped to give the live recordings a much-needed musical boost, beefing up some rather thin arrangements and giving the sound extra texture. Moreover, his importance to the sessions was not lost on the Beatles, who gave him a credit on the label of the 'Get Back'/'Don't Let Me Down' single. He was later to record two fine albums for the Apple label, both of which benefited considerably from George's production and musical imput.

Although George had said he would rejoin the Beatles as long as there was no live concert, we desperately needed some way of bulking out the footage we had already shot. This had become especially important by this point, because after his return to the fold it was decided that the existing footage would not be shown as a 'supporting feature' documentary for a live concert. Rather, it would form the basis of a documentary (or possibly a theatrically released feature film) in its own right.

Everybody thought long and hard about how we could create some kind of musical climax that would demonstrate to fans how the songs that featured in the rehearsals had come to musical fruition. All the spectacular ideas about amphitheatres and ocean liners had long been forgotten, and in the end it was decided, somewhat reluctantly, that the project would be rounded off by a live performance on the roof of the offices. This was a great disappointment to me and seemed such a small idea for the world's biggest group. It was the easiest option and, in the end, something of a compromise. After all, although the show would take place where it could be heard by the public, its location was, ultimately, private. In fact, the only people to witness it were a few Apple employees, the film crew and a handful of city-dwellers who scaled the nearby rooftops to catch a glimpse of the superstars as they performed for the cameras.

There was a palpable air of tension as the group prepared to make what would turn out to be their last concert performance. It reminded me of the bullring performance in Madrid some four years before, although on that night they knew that they would be appearing come hell or high water, whereas this time everything was much less certain. There was no contract that said they had to play; no manager to goad them on to the stage; no hordes of expectant fans to cheer them as they arrived. In fact, given the weeks of arguments and rankling that preceded the show, the film crew (and probably the Beatles themselves) were vaguely surprised and relieved that it happened at all.

The simplicity of the set-up and the fact that they were not in a public place made the shooting easy, despite the fact that I was unable to provide Paul with clearance for a helicopter to get some additional aerial footage. It was impossible to obtain permission for such a stunt at short notice, although doubtless it would have been regarded as a potential hazard anyway. Considering the slothfulness of much of the rehearsals, the concert performance was nothing if not inspired, the Beatles delivering great versions of the songs that they had been rehearsing so unhappily over the previous weeks.[2] Listening to the tapes today, it is hard not to be a little moved by them. It was as if, for the forty-minute duration of the concert, all the tribulations of the previous weeks had been cast aside for the greater good of the group. At this late stage there were many days when things didn't work, but there were also days when that indefinable magic spark that set the Beatles apart from many of their contemporaries would ignite and burn with an awesome intensity that matched and at times exceeded that of their early years. In a way the performance realized and fulfilled the promise of the original idea. In the process, they reminded all of us who were there just why they were so big.

The Beatles will long be remembered for a great many things. I wonder, though, if they'll be remembered for their extraordinary prowess as a live band. This is probably due to the fact that the sound-tracks of most of the footage of their performances is so overwhelmed by teenage screaming that it is impossible to hear much in the way of music. In one respect, it was probably a blessing in disguise that the rooftop performance was restricted in terms of its audience. After all, although none of us knew it at the time, this concert would be the only document of a live Beatles performance where the group could actually be heard!

When they were in the mood for it, they were truly astonishing live. And they were certainly on form for that concert on the roof, their adrenaline spurring them to play with an authority that had been absent from the rehearsals. In the midst of all the disagreement and apathy the concert was a timely reminder to all those who worked with them or for them of why we put up with so much.

After the concert there were a few loose ends to tie up. For a start, the Beatles had to record and shoot some footage of another three songs that were fully rehearsed but had been deemed inappropriate for the rooftop concert. It was also necessary to beef up the finished film with some polished performances. So on 31 January, the day after the live appearance on the roof, the Beatles returned to their Apple basement studios to perform the three numbers.

The songs, 'Let It Be', 'The Long and Winding Road' and 'Two of Us', were all, unsurprisingly, McCartney compositions. All three were memorable in their own way. 'Two of Us' was a pretty, poetic tribute to Linda with a simple, gentle, almost folksy arrangement. Rising to the occasion, John contributed some excellent backing vocals to the song, which encourages some listeners incorrectly to interpret the lyrics as referring to John's and Paul's relationship. Both 'The Long and Winding Road' and 'Let It Be' showcased Paul doing what he did best:

writing ballads with astonishingly beautiful melodies and mass appeal that were somehow romantic without being sentimental, moving without being maudlin, familiar without being clichéd.

Over the years it has become fashionable for critics to knock ten bells out of the songs performed during the 'Get Back' sessions, claiming that they were the low point of the Beatles' career and making unfavourable comparisons with other work from the same era. This is, of course, entirely unfair. To be sure, the rehearsals for the performances could hardly be considered harmonious, and it is true that the Twickenham sessions produced little of great worth. It is also true that John was barely functioning as a member of the band at this point. But disharmony does not always make for a poor finished product, as the project was eventually to testify. In some ways it is not unreasonable to claim the 'Get Back' sessions as a highpoint of Paul's career with the Beatles.[3] Surely any project that can boast songs of the calibre of 'Two of Us', 'Get Back', 'The Long and Winding Road' and 'Let It Be' has to be afforded due respect. Perhaps some of the criticism is owing to the fact that much of the good work featured in the film is Paul's. One thing is for sure. If the other Beatles had any criticism of him for goading them into undertaking the project in the first place, they must also acknowledge that in the end it was he who was responsible for most of the memorable musical moments it provided.

So that was effectively the end of 'Get Back', for me at least. I was back at Twickenham with Ringo to continue work on *The Magic Christian*. However, although production on the 'Get Back' project had largely been completed, there was still an aura of lethargy surrounding it, despite the fact that the filming and recording had finished on something of a high. At its completion the Beatles were so disillusioned with the whole thing and with each other that both the film and the LP were shelved indefinitely. Nobody, it seemed, could face the chore of ploughing through the hours of tapes and working them into a presentable package, and the Beatles themselves were in a state of considerable financial and managerial turmoil.

Just two days before the rooftop concert John had met up with the much feared music industry businessman and manager Allen Klein. Klein, a New York accountant, had gained considerable notoriety in the music industry, with a reputation for helping artists by financial troubleshooting and hustling record companies for better royalty deals. He had managed a number of highly successful British acts, including Donovan and the Rolling Stones. He knew that with Brian gone the Beatles lacked a single management figure and was doubtless aware of John's comments to the press that Apple was losing money and that the Beatles were going broke.

Klein had approached John on a previous occasion but had been unsuccessful in making contact, John later maintaining that he was too nervous to take the call. Now, however, Klein's timing was flawless, and a meeting was arranged over dinner at a suite in London's Dorchester Hotel. A stickler for preparation, he had done his homework, flattering John with his knowledge of Beatles songs and tuning in perfectly to his 'underdog' sympathies. There was an immediate rapport, and they found they shared similar working-class roots and a blunt, acerbic humour. After dinner John, ever impulsive, sat down with Klein and wrote a letter to Joe Lockwood, president of EMI. It simply said, 'Dear Sir Joe, I've asked Allen Klein to look after my things. Please give him any information he wants and full cooperation. Love, John Lennon.'

Despite its casual, off-the-cuff tone, that letter had great significance. It effectively signposted the beginning of the terminal disagreement that would break up the Beatles. In the weeks and months that followed John would persuade George and Ringo that Klein could offer the Beatles the managerial help they needed. Paul, who favoured his future father-in-law Lee Eastman and Eastman's son John – both accomplished and highly respected lawyers – was outvoted three to one. An uneasy amnesty was struck for a time, with Klein renegotiating the Beatles' finances and the Eastmans overseeing his dealings, but it was clear that they would never be able to work with each other in any kind of productive way, as their personalities and approaches were entirely different. Klein was aggressive and forceful, the Eastmans were more used to employing tact and diplomacy in their legal dealings. Klein was given control of the Beatles' fortunes and instructed to 'sort out the mess' at Apple, by saving money where it could be saved and making it where it could be made.

And that's just what he did. His economy boost was straightforward enough and mainly involved firing members of the office staff, regardless of the loyalty they had shown their employers. For example, Alastair, the office manager who had worked first for Brian and then the Beatles for the best part of a decade, was mercilessly given his marching orders. Peter Asher, who had introduced James Taylor to Apple, and Ron Kass, who had played a major part in establishing the records division, could no longer tolerate the atmosphere and left, taking James Taylor with them. Magic Alex either left or was sacked, and an army of secretaries were also dismissed. Derek tolerated the situation for a while longer but eventually left, while Peter Brown and Neil, although probably in the firing line, were given a reprieve as they were so vital to the Beatles' affairs and seemed to pose no immediate threat to Klein's position.

In retrospect, John's comments to the press seemed like a cry for help at a time when Apple was certainly operating in an extremely inefficient manner, largely as a result of the group's open-handedness and idealism. Money flowed out of the organization in a number of ways. To begin with, a great deal of capital was lost on ventures such as the Apple Boutique, The Fool and Apple Electronics. None had turned over any significant profit, and all had received considerable investment from Apple.

Moreover, it is true that there were a number of people both within the organization and peripheral to it who took the Beatles and Apple for granted. And a great deal of money was blown on entertaining journalists, friends and other hangers-on. All of this has been well documented by Richard Dilello, Derek's assistant and Apple's 'house hippy', in his book *The Longest Cocktail Party*. Much of this was indirectly encouraged by the Beatles themselves and resulted from the fact that members of the group, with the possible exception of Paul, were not interested in the day-to-day running of the company. That in itself should not have been a problem, since in more conventional firms line managers are responsible for controlling day-to-day expenditure. But in Apple's early incarnation no such person existed, partly because of organizational inefficiency and partly because the open-handed hippy ethos of the time meant that employing such a business-minded individual would have clashed with the philanthropic ideals on which the company was founded. It was the perfect breeding ground for inefficiency, self-indulgence and massive personal over-expenditure, as every long-lost 'friend', opportunistic journalist and sycophantic wannabe pop star came to eat, drink and smoke at the Beatles' table, despite the fact that their generous benefactors were rarely there. It's not for me to point fingers and blow whistles on individuals, but if Apple was, in part, an idealistic experiment to prove that open-handed ideals, trust and goodwill would be self-perpetuating within the 'enlightened' and alternative anti-materialist sub-culture of hippy-dom, then one can only conclude that it failed miserably.

A key factor in the parlous financial state of the company was, indeed, its philanthropic aims. A great deal of money was lost in attempting to deal with the piles of tapes, film scripts, novels and letters from aspiring artists that poured in daily through the office doors. As well as the cost of employing script readers and so on, the massive administrative problems that this caused jammed up communication channels and generally caused the offices to run inefficiently. Of course, it all would have been worth it if Apple had indeed been a breeding ground for new talent and discovered a new William Goldman or Alfred Hitchcock. But in all of my years in the film industry I have never come across a writer or director who was discovered via an unsolicited manuscript or letter. I wish that weren't true, but it is.

Yet although Apple lacked an efficient structure, John's fears of 'being broke in six months' were somewhat exaggerated, for while money was flowing out of Apple it was also flowing in. Although nobody could pretend that *Magical Mystery Tour* had been a major commercial success, it had still been highly profitable. More importantly, the Apple record label had released some remarkably bankable product. Not least of these were the 'White Album' and the 'Hey Jude' single, which at the time were among the fastest-selling and most successful records ever made.

Of course, it is true that Apple lost money in its infancy, and there can be no questioning the fact that a considerable amount of capital was squandered. But one has to bear in mind the fact that it takes significant time and effort from both employees and directors for any entertainment company to get up and running. Major organizations, especially those with such lofty ideals and all-encompassing objectives as Apple, cannot be expected to go into profit the moment they are established. All companies need a teething period before they really get going. If Apple had been just a record label, the situation might have been different, but that wasn't what the Beatles, or any of us, wanted it to be.

I look back at that first incarnation of the company with a mixture of pride and despair: pride because I feel that in some ways Apple was an exceptionally innovative organization which can now be seen as a forerunner to successful companies such as Virgin or Chrysalis that have followed similar diverse (but synergetic) aspirations; despair because the company was so inefficiently managed that we never got the chance to see our ideas through in the way we had envisaged. Given another two years, Apple could perhaps have become a fantastic breeding ground for new talent and the first major British company successfully to invest in music, film and publishing all at once. If it had not been for the fruitless and naïve methods of trying to discover new talent, the unacceptable drains on the company's finances and a non-existent system of man management, it could have been a huge international success. But the Beatles were not in a position to help anyone.

They were not in a position to help themselves, and, at a time when solidarity, open-mindedness and communication were the keys to their professional salvation, there was nothing but disagreement, delusion and dead air.

Some six weeks after the Apple sessions for the 'Get Back' film were completed, the Beatles finally redirected their attention to the project, if only from a cautious distance. Still feeling unable to trawl through the tapes themselves, they asked engineer Glyn Johns to compile an LP, and between May and June 1969 the Beatles came close to releasing the soundtrack album of 'Get Back'. The cover, which was intended to signify their circular return to rock and roll, famously pictured the group in the same pose that had graced the cover of their first LP, *Please Please Me*, looking down from the stairwell of EMI's building in London's Manchester Square. The cover shot was, at John's request, taken by photographer Angus McBean, who had been responsible for the picture on the first album. The 'Get Back' sleeve also emulated the typography of *Please Please Me*, stating that it featured 'Let It Be' and eleven other songs.

I thought it was an excellent package and that Glyn had done a good job, retaining the rawness and excitement that was supposed to have been the *raison d'être* of the sessions. As many fans know, the ill-fated 'Get Back' LP boasted a very different track-listing to the final, rechristened, remixed and recompiled *Let It Be* album. It included such tracks as a jam of the Drifters' 'Save the Last Dance for Me', a short McCartney instrumental called 'Rocker', a version of John's 'Don't Let Me Down' ballad and Paul's quaint little throwaway 'Teddy Boy', which he later rerecorded for *McCartney*, his first post-Beatles solo album. But the group was not happy with it, and the album was temporarily scrapped.

Some time later, in January 1970, Glyn, under instructions from the Beatles, completed work on another version, but this, too, failed to

159

meet with approval from all four who, as usual, couldn't agree on whether they liked it or not and ended up rejecting it. Obviously, they were somewhat bored with the music and were therefore not really in the mood to listen to endless remixes and compilations, but this was just part of the problem. Although the Beatles themselves had come up with the idea of making a 'warts and all' LP with a minimum of over-dubbing and studio trickery, I think they got cold feet when it came to putting out the results of the experiment. It was as if, after years of producing polished studio LPs, they couldn't bear to be seen 'naked' musically, to put out an album that was so different from the records that preceded it during the studio years after they stopped playing live. If this is true, it's a great shame, as anyone who has heard either of the much-bootlegged 'Get Back' compilations will tell you.

The only recording that was released in the immediate aftermath of the filming was the single 'Get Back'/'Don't Let Me Down', which was issued in April 1969. Another McCartney A-side, 'Get Back', which its writer described as 'music to rollercoast to', was an enormous hit throughout the world. Its flip-side, John's 'Don't Let Me Down', was equally strong although less obviously commercial. A blues-influenced mantra to Yoko, it can be seen as a precursor to the powerful 'I Want You', which would close the first side of the Beatles last LP, *Abbey Road*.

By the time the renamed *Let It Be* film and album eventually sur-faced, a great deal more water would have passed under the bridge and the world's most successful pop group would have ceased to exist.

NNNN   LGS 216G

ZGZG LLG2493 NLA445
SWARGASHRAM 25 13 1440

DENIS O DELLAPPLE FILMS 95 WIGMORE STLONDON W1 ENGLAND

COME TO ACADEMY RISHIKESH ASSOON AS POSSIBLE
FILM DEALS BEING NEGOTIATED URGENT LOVE FROM THE
BEATLES

COL 0 95 W1

The telegram from the Beatles
asking me to join them in India in spring 1968

Paul in reflective mood,
Rishikesh, India, 1968
© Denis O'Dell

With Paul and Neil Aspinall
in Rishikesh
© Denis O'Dell

Paul in India
© Denis O'Dell

It was a great privilege to watch Paul composing songs that would eventually make their way on to the 'White Album'.
© Denis O'Dell

Unsurprisingly, George spent much of his time in India developing his skills with the sitar.

© *Denis O'Dell*

Jane Asher also has a go

© *Denis O'Dell*

George plays air guitar
while Jane gets sore fingers.
© Denis O'Dell

Paul composing on the roof of
the Maharishi's ashram

© Denis O'Dell

Paul and Jane never did take my advice!

© Denis O'Dell

Neil accompanied me from New Delhi
to the ashram.
© *Denis O'Dell*

His divine holiness, Neil Aspinall!
© *Denis O'Dell*

Paul, Jane and other guests hang
loose at the ashram bungalows.
© *Denis O'Dell*

The Maharishi's Academy of
Transcendental Meditation in
Rishikesh, by the Ganges
© *Denis O'Dell*

Two views of the Maharishi's
ashram in Rishikesh, 1968
© *Denis O'Dell*

Hello, goodbye! Paul, Jane and Neil

© *Denis O'Dell*

Bramacharya Rhaghwendra (far right) was a close aide of the Maharishi.

© Denis O'Dell

Paul sporting a classic pair of sixties sidies
© Denis O'Dell

George enjoys a natural high.
© *Denis O'Dell*

Patti Boyd
© *Denis O'Dell*

Dear Prudence

© *Denis O'Dell*

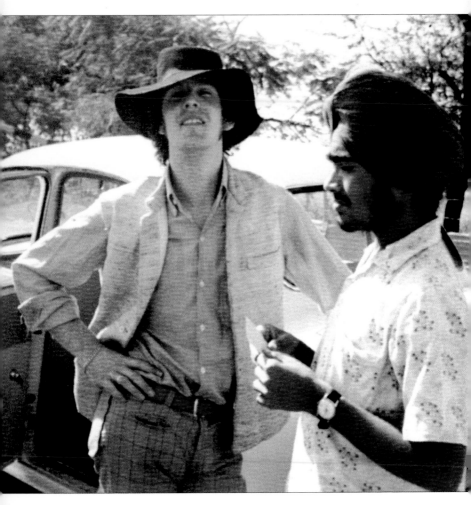

Neil with our driver

© *Denis O'Dell*

Me wandering round town and by the Ganges

© *Denis O'Dell*

The wisdom is the light of God
from within dear blessed Denis
O'Dell. Enjoy and radiate
the joy for all to enjoy.

Inscriptions by the Maharishi
in *The Science of Being and
the Art of Living* and the
Bhagavad-Gita, given to me
in India

The song of life sung
by the Lord is to be sung
dear blessed Denis O'Dell
so that the echo rings
for generations to come.
Enjoy.

11

Carry On Till Tomorrow

WHILE THE BEATLES were busy trying to get their act together at Twickenham, I was working flat out on the pre-production of the film version of Terry Southern's classic satire *The Magic Christian*. For some years I had been a friend of Scottish television and film producer and director Joe McGrath. To some extent we moved in similar circles. He was a friend of Richard Lester's and had been involved in one or two Beatles-related projects. As well as directing the group in their first promo clips in 1965, he had a hand in preparing screen treatments for *Help!* the same year. The year before he had contributed one or two minor ideas for visual gags to *A Hard Day's Night*. He had also been the producer of Peter Cook's and Dudley Moore's classic television comedy series *Not Only . . . But Also . . .*, which had featured cameo appearances from John Lennon. The first of these, in 1965, was a sketch with John reading excerpts from *In His Own Write*. The second and most memorable occurred the following year and featured Lennon as a lavatory attendant in a bizarre piece of surreal comedy shot outside the gents' toilets in Soho's Broadwick Street. This was the first time the public had seen John's new image, minus the Beatle mop-top hairstyle and sporting the famous National Health Service-style 'granny glasses' that would become his visual trademark from then on.

Joe had long been interested in doing more work with the Beatles, with whom he maintained a sound if not close relationship. He and I were good friends, and he would often drop in at the Apple offices to say hello or chat about whatever projects we were developing at the time. One day, in mid-1968, he stopped by to discuss an idea that I thought had enormous promise and which could be highly profitable for us both.

As a film and TV producer/director Joe had good connections, particularly in the world of comedy. Over the years he had worked with a great many of Britain's major comedy stars, including legendary comic actor and former Goon Peter Sellers. Joe explained that Peter and he had discussed the possibility of making a film version of *The Magic Christian*. Although the adaptation of Southern's novel *Candy* – which starred Marlon Brando and featured a cameo from Ringo – was not a huge critical or commercial success, the writer was regarded as a great satirist in the USA. Moreover, his scriptwriting skills would the same year help to make *Easy Rider* one of the most successful independent movies of all time.[1]

The book of *The Magic Christian* concerns the exploits of an immensely wealthy and eccentric businessman, Sir Guy Grand. His surreal sense of humour and insatiable curiosity about human avarice and greed lead him to conduct a number of entertaining experiments in which he seeks to prove that there is absolutely nothing that mankind will not do for material gain. In that first discussion Joe told me that Peter was interested in getting the film together as a vehicle for himself as Guy Grand. However, he felt that in the film version Guy should have an adopted son, a waif whom he would befriend in the opening scenes and who would provide a perfect comic foil for Grand's eccentric antics. Peter was a great admirer of the Beatles, and I think Joe had mentioned to him that they, or Apple Films, might be interested in discussing such a venture. So shortly after Joe's initial visit a meeting was arranged between Joe, Peter and myself.

Peter was keen to get the project off the ground and wished to involve the Beatles. He originally wanted John to play Sir Guy's adopted son Youngman Grand. Although I was sceptical over that particular piece of casting, I certainly didn't think it would do Apple Films' reputation any harm to get involved in a production with one of the most bankable and respected comedy stars in the world. I didn't think John would be interested though, as he hadn't particularly enjoyed making *How I Won the War* and was so involved with Yoko that I couldn't envisage him committing himself to a starring role in a major movie. I suggested Ringo instead. I argued, first of all, that he was a better actor, and, second, he was far more likely to be up for it. We agreed that I would approach him and that we should really start to develop the film, with Joe directing, Peter starring and myself producing. Terry was brought in to adapt his novel for the screen.

The novel had been written a decade earlier and needed updating, adapting for the cinema and making more visually arresting. As a result, many of Guy Grand's increasingly bizarre psychological experiments were either altered or changed entirely for the film. These included bribing the Oxford boat crew to cheat and rig the result of the annual Oxford and Cambridge Boat Race, a parking warden, played by Spike Milligan, eating a ticket for a vast cash reward and, in the final sequence, Sir Guy floating vast amounts of cash in a vat of animal manure, urine and pigs' blood to find out whether city businessmen would be prepared to 'take the plunge' to retrieve the booty. This being a Terry Southern satire, they do. Another major alteration was the Anglicization of the story, which had originally been set in the USA. Peter wanted to play Guy Grand as an Englishman, and this was the late sixties and London was the epicentre of Western popular culture. Such an approach would, of course, be unheard of today.

One of my original hopes was that the film could be produced through Apple. However, Peter had his own film production company, Delegate Films, and we eventually agreed that we would form an offshoot of this company, Grand Films, to develop and make the picture. In autumn 1968 I arranged a business lunch with Ringo at a local pub around the corner from the Apple offices and offered him the role. As I had anticipated, he was extremely receptive to the proposal, as he was keen to develop his acting skills and was a friend of Terry's following his role in *Candy* earlier in the year. He was also a huge fan of

Peter's, and the chance to share equal billing with a former Goon and major international star proved irresistible. We now had what appeared to be a very tempting package with which to approach distributors for funding: a highly respected director, a major international film star, a story based on an acclaimed novel and a Beatle.

Our first port of call was Columbia Pictures. Despite my good contacts within the company and my confidence in the package, we were turned down flat. The problem, they said, was Peter. Although he seemed perfectly affable to me, his reputation for being a prima donna bothered Columbia, despite his box office bankability, and they rejected the film on that basis. We then approached Commonwealth United Films, an international distribution company, arranging a meeting in Paris with one of its directors, Oliver Unger. Peter didn't come, but Joe and I managed to convince Unger of the film's potential profitability, and we got ourselves around £3.5 million with which to finance the picture.

Meanwhile Terry and Joe continued work on the screenplay, Anglicizing, modernizing and adapting, frantically writing in Ringo's role as Youngman and generally trying to get the thing into some sort of filmable shape. They did a pretty good job, I think, although when Peter saw the first draft of the screenplay he felt that it needed an additional boost and brought in future Python stars John Cleese and Graham Chapman to contribute to the script. They were to feature in the movie, too, albeit in minor roles, with Chapman playing an Oxford stroke and Cleese appearing as a Sotheby's auctioneer who sells a Rembrandt portrait to Sir Guy who then proceeds to cut out the only part of the portrait that he collects – the nose. This, of course, was pure Python-style surrealism. The film was shot just as the Monty Python team were forming, and *The Magic Christian* marked the first of many projects that would later, in one way or another, unite members of both. This was fitting really, since Python were to do for British comedy what the Beatles had done for pop.[2]

Shooting for the film finally began at Twickenham in February

1969, shortly after the 'Get Back' footage from the previous month was completed. Although we had a decent budget from Commonwealth and knew that the movie had great potential, we felt that it would be fun and an added commercial draw to include some cameo appearances from major stars.

Raquel Welch was the first person that we approached. In the original screenplay she was to play a scantily clad dominatrix who would whip a galleyful of male slaves into shape. I sent the script over to her, not sure if she would be amenable to the idea and was pleased to find that she was. A week or so before her scene was due to be shot she came over to the studio for a costume fitting. Being a producer can be a tough job, but I felt it was my responsibility to attend the fitting, just to make sure that everything was OK. I'm pleased to say that it was, and she looked absolutely stunning. A couple of days later, one Saturday morning, Joe, Terry and I were discussing progress when I asked them, half jokingly, what they thought about replacing the male slaves in Raquel's scene with a crew of topless models. This would obviously not be considered politically correct these days, but times change and I wasn't the first producer in the world to reason that a bit of gratuitous sex never did the box office any harm. Joe and Terry, however, were aghast.

'Bloody hell, Denis, she'd never do it . . . Would she?'

There was only one way to find out.

Without Raquel's knowledge we recruited around thirty topless models to 'man' the galley on the day of Raquel's shooting and prayed that when she turned up for work she would be good-humoured about it all and not walk out. Just in case I had arranged an emergency dominatrix to replace her. Luckily Raquel took it all in her stride and was totally at ease with the situation, even when Terry called for 'extra nipple distension' and had prop men distribute ice cubes to the galley slaves!

Raquel's cameo inspired us to try to persuade more major stars to appear in the film. I managed to get Laurence Harvey and Christopher

Lee, as well as Roman Polanski and Yul Brynner, who memorably appeared in drag singing 'Mad About the Boy' to Polanski in the ship's cabaret bar before revealing himself as a man. Yul was initially somewhat reluctant at first to appear as a woman, which was unsurprising given the macho image he had cultivated so assiduously in films such as *The Magnificent Seven*. However, after some persuasion I managed to get him to try on the costume in my office and he eventually agreed. In fact, both he and Polanski entered into the spirit of the film with great gusto, and the scene was tremendous fun to shoot. Financier Louis J. Nicastro was visiting the set on the day that this particular scene was shot and burst into fits of laughter when Yul removed his wig, forcing us to reshoot the scene. We didn't really mind. It was his money after all!

That scene was, however, to lead to one of the most embarrassing incidents of my career. After the film was completed and cut I attended a certification screening of the film with John Trevelyan, then head of British Film Classification. We sat down together to watch the movie, which Trevelyan seemed to be enjoying. When the 'Mad About the Boy' scene commenced and Yul started his seductive song routine, Trevelyan turned to me and whispered, 'Good God, she's interesting!' At that moment Yul removed his wig and revealed himself as a man. Trevelyan's face contorted indescribably and I sat there frozen with embarrassment, hoping that when the most powerful man in the British film industry had stopped looking shamefacedly at the floor he wouldn't give us an 'X' rating!

I remember the shooting of the film with great fondness. There was a truly happy and cooperative atmosphere for the most part, and Ringo worked very well with all the cast and crew. He had come on in leaps and bounds as an actor and was keen to learn all he could from Peter, who was generally very supportive, and the two developed a close friendship over the course of the shoot. In fact, Ringo's practical and unassuming personality was an ideal foil for Peter, who could be given to some pretty difficult behaviour at times.

Columbia's worries about Peter's temperament proved well founded; he could be very tricky to deal with. I liked him immensely, but as I came to know him better I discovered at first hand his extremely volatile disposition, for he was a man capable of the most extraordinary mood swings. One moment he was the closest and most generous friend you could ever hope to encounter, the next he was like a spoilt child, acting up because he hadn't got his way.

Saturdays have always been sacrosanct to me. Film productions notwithstanding, if I could avoid working on a Saturday I did, as Donna and I used to take a great interest in horse-racing and would always attend the race meetings at which we had one of our own horses entered. One such Saturday we were walking out of the house to drive to Sandown Park racecourse when the phone rang.

'Denis, it's Peter.'

I could tell immediately by his flat and empty tone of voice that something was terribly, terribly wrong.

'Peter, what's the matter?'

'That's it. I'm going to end it.'

'What are you talking about?'

'I've had a terrible argument with Michael, and that's it, I'm going to end it all.' Michael was Peter's son.

'You can't do that, Peter. You can't do that to your son. No matter what his shortcomings are – or yours. You simply can't do that to your own son.'

I suggested to him that he come with us to the races to try to take his mind off things, but he wasn't interested. There was no way that I could get over to see him before the race meeting, so I suggested that he rest on it and, after a great deal of persuasion, he agreed to come and have dinner with us that evening. I was obviously very concerned for him but figured that if Peter had some kind of appointment it would keep him together until we had the chance to discuss his problems further.

On returning home we awaited his arrival with some trepidation,

167

assuming that he would be in a dreadfully depressed state. Remarkably, however, he arrived for dinner in excellent spirits, and Donna and I spent a wonderful evening being regaled with hilarious stories and anecdotes as only Peter could tell them. He didn't once mention his problems with Michael or the fact that eight hours earlier he had contemplated suicide. In fact, I honestly think that he had forgotten all about it.

What made him like this I don't know. For what it's worth, I think his main problem was that he didn't seem to have any clear sense of his own identity. This resulted in a personality that could not always distinguish whether he was acting in character or behaving normally. There were times off the set when one would witness him transforming from his usual self (whatever that was) into a different character of his own creation.

Once, for example, Joe, Peter and myself were returning to London from a recce in the country, looking at potential locations for the film. As we were driving through Muswell Hill, Peter suddenly changed into a plummy-voiced London estate agent, attempting to talk up various properties that we passed, staying in character for the remaining thirty minutes of the journey. The voice sounded strangely familiar, and as he continued, I had an odd feeling of *déjà vu*. I had definitely heard that voice before and not just an approximation of it. Whoever's voice it was, it was an exact copy. Eventually, as we came to the end of our journey, it clicked. The man Peter was mimicking was a real London estate agent, a Mr Slinn, based in Muswell Hill. I had done some business with him many years earlier. The impression was unmistakable and impeccable.

'Peter, I know who that is.'

He looked surprised. 'Who what is?'

'That voice. I know it. It's an estate agent from here called Mr Slinn.'

He was taken aback. 'How on earth did you know that?' he asked, incredulous.

'I bought my first house from him.'

'Really? That *is* a coincidence.'

I looked at him, puzzled.

'I bought one off him, too!'

Peter's ability to mimic was beyond remarkable, and he would frequently transform himself into another person so suddenly and so completely that you would be left dumbstruck with a combination of admiration and unease. It was as if he was 'trying characters on', much as you or I might try on hats. With Peter the boundaries of fact and fiction, of real and unreal and of work and leisure were never clearly defined and, indeed, for those who knew him they were constantly blurred.

Whether this was born out of his preoccupation with acting, whether he had some kind of personality disorder or whether he simply had a surreal sense of humour I cannot say. Perhaps it was all of these, perhaps none. I spent a considerable amount of time with him in the late sixties and early seventies. For a couple of years I probably saw as much of him as any other person in the film world did, but he was a truly impossible character to get to know well, since you never knew which Peter Sellers you would encounter on any given occasion. The man who would at one moment fire a crew member for wearing the wrong-coloured clothing might two minutes later be full of goodwill and praise for his fellow actors. I hate to trot out old clichés, but perhaps the one about there being a thin line between genius and madness is applicable to Peter. I have certainly never met anybody quite like him since. I'm not sure whether to be thankful for that or not.

Joe knew all about Peter's changeable personality of old, having worked with him before on a number of occasions. In fact, Peter had fired Joe as director from Charles Feldman's extravagant and unofficial James Bond spoof *Casino Royale* in 1967. Although Peter was pleased to have Joe directing *The Magic Christian*, the latter was well aware of the potential for problems to recur. The actor was an enormous power on any film and, since it was his company that had developed and were effectively producing the movie, it was obvious that he could fire anyone who crossed him.

When the film was still in pre-production Joe came to my offices to discuss the potential pitfalls of working with Peter.

'You know, Denis, he's a great guy, but he isn't easy to deal with,' he told me. 'He always fires people for one reason or another. He'll almost certainly try to fire me or you at some point during the shoot.' At this stage I barely knew Peter, and he had seemed perfectly civil, if a little eccentric. I was aware of his reputation, however, and certainly didn't want to risk being fired at whim by anyone. Joe then proposed an idea to me that could make our positions on the production a great deal more secure. He suggested that we add a clause to our contracts which stipulated if either of us was fired the other would have to go at the same time. In other words, we would tie our contracts together. This was unheard of at the time and was an enormous gamble. However, we felt that, on balance, it was unlikely that Peter would attempt to fire us both simultaneously and that such a scheme would therefore be more likely to help than hinder us. The contracts were duly drawn up.

It was a good thing, too. Sure enough, a few weeks after shooting commenced Peter requested a private lunch with me in his dressing-room at the studios. Although nothing major had gone wrong, the shooting had started a little shakily, and I knew from the actor's tone that he had something serious on his mind. I arrived at his room, and he immediately dropped the bombshell.

'Denis, I want to fire Joe.'

I sighed to myself. Joe had been absolutely right. 'Well, Peter,' I said, 'that's fine. I should tell you, though, that if you fire Joe I'll be contractually bound to go as well.'

He listened, dumbfounded, as I explained the tied contracts to him. I didn't, of course, tell him *why* Joe and I had come to this arrangement and, although he had never been confronted with such a situation before, I think I caught a glint of suspicion in his eye, a look that said, 'You crafty old sod!' He didn't, however, want to fire me as well.

'In that case,' he said, 'I want to stop the picture.'

This is serious, I thought. This mustn't be allowed to happen.

'OK, Peter,' I told him evenly, 'but you must understand that if we stop the production your company will have to pay Commonwealth for all the shooting costs we've incurred so far.'

He fixed a piercing stare at me.

'At the moment,' I said, 'these costs are around one and a half million pounds.'

He fixed an even more piercing stare at me, and there was a prolonged silence as I struggled to find something productive to add. I knew the future of the film could depend on how well this was handled.

'Look,' I continued, 'I'm the kind of producer who likes to get problems out in the open. Why don't we get Joe up here and we can discuss any problems you're having between us all.' Although I had only worked with him for a few months, I had learned that Peter was nothing if not temperamental and that, like his moods, his decisions also changed like the wind. I knew – or at least I thought I knew – that if I could keep some kind of dialogue going he would change his mind and want to begin shooting again.

Luckily he agreed to discuss the situation in front of Joe, and I went down to the stage to find the director and tell him what was going on.

He was not in the least surprised. 'Oh, right,' he said, as though he had just been told that his shoelace had come undone or that he had left his car lights on. 'I wondered how long it would be before that happened.' He agreed that we had better talk to Peter and try to pacify him.

Near by on the Twickenham sound stage Ringo and the rest of the cast and crew idly waited around, oblivious to the discussions that were going on in Peter's dressing-room. With no director, star or producer around to keep the film rolling, there was little for the bemused

171

crew to do but await instructions. If we couldn't persuade Peter to reconsider his position, the only instructions anybody would be getting were 'Thank you and goodnight.'

That little incident turned out to be one of the longest lunch breaks I've ever taken, not to mention one of the most expensive, since most of the afternoon's shooting was lost, with the cast and crew on full pay. Fortunately, however, Peter and Joe did manage to iron out their differences and resolve whatever problems they – or Peter – thought they had. I honestly can't remember exactly what the actor claimed was the issue, so it was probably something pretty trivial. It is possible that he just wanted some attention. Anyway, in the end he agreed to carry on with the film, and several hours later the three of us emerged back on the set to resume shooting. When he returned to work Peter was in excellent spirits, joking with the cast and crew as if nothing had happened.

Following this incident the shooting went exceptionally well, and there were no further problems. One of the key reasons for this, I think, was Ringo's personality. He was the ideal person to keep Peter in check. Ringo was more famous, but he had an unassuming and equable outlook on life which could not help but have a calming influence on those around him. Although Peter would never adopt his laid-back attitude to acting, I'm sure the Beatle's presence was beneficial. Even Peter Sellers would have felt ridiculous throwing a tantrum in front of Ringo Starr!

One day Peter invited Princess Margaret on to the set to watch the shooting. As it happened, the day that she came to see her old friend coincided with filming the sequence at the restaurant in which Peter has his dinner of duck à l'orange hurled at him by the waiters. He later quipped that he was one of the few film stars that could claim to have 'thrown lunch' for a Royal!

Although *The Magic Christian* was not an Apple Films production, I figured that it was worth trying to get the other Beatles involved in the soundtrack music. I asked Paul if he would be interested in writing the score for the now completed film. He was not enthusiastic.

Although he had enjoyed working on the soundtrack to *The Family Way* in 1966 (and had won an Ivor Novello award for it), he didn't want to get too involved in writing film music. I asked if it would be possible to use 'Yesterday' in the opening title sequence of the movie, in which Ringo is seen sleeping rough in a park and is discovered by Sir Guy Grand. Understandably, he didn't want us to use his song in such a way. However, he did agree to help out with some of the music, even writing the film's signature tune, 'Come and Get It', which was eventually performed by a newly signed Apple group called the Iveys. They were a discovery of Mal's and at that point something of an unknown quantity. I was initially reluctant to use them, but Paul felt that if he did some of the arrangements and the band were renamed we would be on to a winner.

I am not sure that Paul's naming of the group came directly from 'Badfinger Boogie', the working title of the song 'With a Little Help from My Friends', as received wisdom has it. In 1969 my young son Arran, just a baby at the time, cut his finger on a knife and had an enormous bandage put on his hand. He was fascinated by his wound, as young children often are, and for several days took great pleasure in showing everybody his injury, pointing at it with his good hand and repeating endlessly in baby talk, 'Bad finger, bad finger.' I told Paul about this and he loved the childish exclamation, saying it would make a great name for a pop group. The phrase had obviously been in his head since 1967 when he had used it as the working title for the *Sergeant Pepper* classic, but as far as I'm aware it was this incident with Arran that spurred him into thinking of it as a potential name for a band.

Paul's song, 'Come and Get It', was demoed one day in June 1969 while the Beatles were in the process of recording *Abbey Road*, with its composer playing all of the instruments. Remarkably, it took him just an hour. Paul produced the song and rightly insisted that the original arrangement remain unaltered. Badfinger also recorded a couple of other McCartney-produced tracks that were used in the film, and

Apple Records later released Badfinger's debut LP under the title of *Magic Christian Music*, despite the fact that less than half of the tracks on the LP were featured in the movie. Badfinger, of course, went on to become one of Apple's most interesting signings. During the late sixties and early seventies they chalked up a number of hit albums and singles and produced such memorable songs as 'Day After Day', 'No Matter What' and 'Without You', an enormous hit for Harry Nilsson and, later on, Mariah Carey. They also appeared on a number of solo Beatles material projects, making an appearance on John's 1971 *Imagine* LP, George's *All Things Must Pass* and *The Concert for Bangladesh* albums and Ringo's tremendous single 'It Don't Come Easy'. George later produced a number of songs for their 1972 LP release, *Straight Up*. However, despite the fact that the group have been virtually forgotten in their native UK, their LPs, particularly the brooding *No Dice* (1971) and *Straight Up*, have achieved enormous cult status in the USA. Their deftly crafted melodies and power pop sensibilities closely mirror those of their benefactors and, although some have claimed that their melodic and harmonic structures mirror the Beatles somewhat too closely, this seems rather churlish. The Beatles were, after all, enormously important to Badfinger. As well as indirectly discovering them and producing a number of their records, they were obviously a considerable musical influence. But Badfinger were also talented artists and composers in their own right. The tragic suicides of their two chief songwriters, Pete Ham in 1975 and Tom Evans in 1983, robbed popular music of two very gifted musicians.

After the completion of the film I arranged a huge publicity party at Les Ambassadeurs Club in London. It was one of the most star-studded parties of the decade, and the guest list read like a who's who of contemporary pop culture. As well as all the star names featured in the film, a swathe of the most popular celebrities of the era also attended. Among them were Richard Harris, Roger Moore, Stanley Baker, Sean Connery and of course the recently married couples from the Beatles' camp, John and Yoko and Paul and Linda.

The Magic Christian came in under budget, which may seem surprising given the enormous roll-call of stars. However, most of the
cameos were done for fun and friendship rather than financial remu-
neration. Yul Brynner did his part for expenses only, as did Polanski. I
think we fitted a new kitchen for Laurence Harvey in return for his
superb 'strip Hamlet' performance! The whole enterprise was made in
great spirits, and because the stars didn't take themselves or the film
too seriously the movie had a lightness of touch that I liked immensely.

It's always pleasing to come in under budget when you are producing a picture. Although you strive to meet the challenge of whatever
budget you are working to, it's not always possible, for all sorts of
reasons. I was especially glad that we managed so well on The Magic
Christian, because Louis J. Nicastro had promised that if we did he
would pay for Ringo, Peter, Terry, Joe and myself – and our respective
partners – to take a luxury Atlantic cruise on the newly launched QE2.
He proved to be as good as his word and on 16 May we set off for the
biggest Apple of them all.

12

A Taste of Honey

JOHN AND YOKO were going to join us for the cruise to New York, but because of John's recent drugs conviction he was unable to obtain a visitor's visa from the American immigration authorities. Peter was accompanied by his fiancée Miranda Quarry, Joe brought his partner Peta, Terry came with his young son and his girlfriend Gail, and I was with Donna. Ringo brought along his entire entourage, including his wife Maureen, his children Jason and Zak, their nanny and the family chauffeur Alan. I'm not sure that Louis was too keen on this or why Ringo felt that he needed a chauffeur on a cruise, but no harm was done, and Louis has remained a lifelong friend, becoming the god-father to my youngest daughter Laragh, who was born later that year.

The scale and grandeur of the *QE2* was breathtaking. Longer than three full-sized football pitches and towering fourteen storeys above the water, she was – and is – the world's most famous luxury liner. Inside, the public rooms were decorated in a lavish art-deco style, evoking an almost decadent extravagance. Everything was astonish-ingly luxurious and opulent, and the range of facilities was, at the time, unprecedented. There were casinos, a cinema, several excellent restaurants and sumptuous bars as well as huge lounges that dripped with affluence.

We were given first-class accommodation, and the service was extraordinary. Personal stewards were allocated to each couple, and the quarters were not cabins but suites with their own bathrooms, lounges, bars and bedrooms.

I would like to be able to say that the crossing was an enjoyable one. Certainly what I remember of it was most enjoyable. Unfortunately, I can't remember large chunks of it, courtesy of Peter Sellers.

Shortly after we boarded the boat, Peter invited me to some pre-dinner drinks in his cabin.

'Ah, Sir Guy! So glad to see you,' he said in his best clipped English accent as I arrived at his quarters. For some reason he had taken to calling me Sir Guy, even though it was the name of the character he played in *The Magic Christian*. His luxurious suite had a beautiful bar and a wonderful spread of canapés on it, many of which seemed to contain honey. We were due to meet the others in half an hour for dinner, so I didn't really want to eat or drink too much, but everything was beautifully presented and Peter was insistent that I indulge.

'Dear boy, you must at least try the canapés! I made them myself, you know!'

And so I did. They were quite delicious. Unfortunately I spent the rest of the evening with my head spinning in a kind of bewildered although hugely pleasant daze. Everything that happened seemed to take an eternity. It was as though I were watching everything, all inter-action, as if it had been taped and then replayed in slow motion. My voice didn't feel like it belonged to me. It was detached, separated somehow from its owner, as though it was emanating from some distant and poorly tuned radio. After the most wonderful dinner of duck à l'orange (the favoured food of Sir Guy Grand in the film), we went off to the ship's cinema to see a film, although I've no idea what we saw.

I was basically out of it for three of the five days that we were on the boat. Later Peter told me that the honey on the canapés was not the stuff that you find in your local supermarket. This was his 'special' honey. According to him, it was made by bees fed on pure opium. He took a dozen jars of it into the USA. I suppose it's not the kind of thing that you get frisked for at customs!

'Don't, whatever you do, try Peter's finger food,' I warned Ringo and Terry some time later.

The cruise was tremendous fun, and Ringo was in great spirits throughout. I think *The Magic Christian* came at just the right time in his career, at a point in his life when he most needed something other than the Beatles on which to concentrate.

After the honey incident Peter was his usual enigmatic and contrary self. On the last evening of the cruise, just before we arrived in New York, he phoned down to my quarters. 'What are you doing, Sir Guy?' he enquired, still in upper-class Englishman mode.

'Well, Peter, I was just about to head up to the ship's bar to have me a glass of champagne.'

'D'you know, I think I'll join you!'

We met up at the Midship's Bar five minutes later. Peter's volatile personality was evident once more. Within those few minutes he had changed from affable toff to taciturn philosopher. We ordered our drinks and sat down together in silence.

Peter stared into space, then looked at me very seriously. 'You're a man of the world, Sir Guy.'

I nodded uncertainly, unsure what was coming next.

'I need some advice.' There was an uneasy pause. 'If you wished to put an end to a long-standing relationship, what would you do?'

Where is this leading? I wondered to myself. I thought for a while. He was clearly referring to Miranda, I figured, who was with us on the boat.

'Well, Peter,' I said, choosing my words as carefully as I could, 'I think that the most healthy thing in those circumstances is to put distance between yourself and the person that you are trying to split up with.'

There was a short silence as he took in what I had just said, and then a little knowing smile gradually spread across his face.

'Ah, yes. Distance. You know, old chap, that's a very good answer. A very good answer indeed.'

We talked some more, but that was the last time the subject was mentioned.

The following year Peter and Miranda were married.

*

Five days after the QE2 set sail, we arrived in New York and had a wonderful Chinese meal with Louis, after which we stayed at the luxurious Carlyle Hotel in Manhattan for the night. Peter and Miranda flew off to Los Angeles the next day, while the rest of us took a plane to the Bahamas, where we stayed for a few relaxing days, lazing around and deep-sea fishing on Paradise Island. While we were there, our group was invited for lunch by the American tycoon Huntington Hartford, a millionaire and owner of Paradise Island who had a palatial Bahamian mansion by the sea. With its vast stretches of isolated golden beach and luxurious décor, Huntington's house was probably one of the most desirable properties in the world.

We sat down to enjoy a splendid lunch, as Huntington, a charming host, regaled us with stories about the island. After an informal alfresco meal we spent the day enjoying his hospitality and swimming in the calm blue waters. I assumed that the main reason for our host's invitation was to meet Ringo. Although Terry was an internationally recognized writer, Ringo was the world-famous celebrity of our little group. Yet although Huntington was impeccably well mannered throughout our visit I got the distinct feeling that he wasn't really making much of an effort to speak to the Beatle. In fact I couldn't help noticing that he spent the majority of the next two hours talking intensely about his house to Alan. This struck me as slightly odd. Alan was a very nice man, but I wasn't aware that he had any particular interest in or knowledge of Bahamian architecture or interior design. How refreshing, I thought, that a man of such wealth and status should be so unaffected as to spend the evening talking to a chauffeur.

Following a highly enjoyable day we thanked our host for his hospitality and returned to our hotel. It later transpired that Huntington desperately wanted to sell his beautiful house and had spent the entire evening talking to Alan under the misapprehension that he was Ringo's business manager. It never emerged whether the sale was one of the main reasons for our invitation, but, if it was, he was certainly talking to the wrong man. However, I heard some time later that he sold the house to Richard Harris, so he must have struck lucky in the end.

On returning to the UK prospects looked very bright indeed for *The Magic Christian*; so bright that after one of the publicity screenings in the USA I received a phone call in the UK at three in the morning from Oliver Unger at Commonwealth Films. I was to be given some very good news. Responses to the film on the test screenings had been very positive. The movie was set to become a monster – and if commercial audiences responded the way that the trial ones had done it might just prove to be the most successful film of the decade. Furthermore, with the fortune I was set to earn from my cut of the film's profits I would be well advised to get out of Britain where the bulk of my earnings would be taken by the taxman.

When you've been in the film industry for a good many years you get used to the smell of bullshit. 'It's going to make this; it's going to win that; it's going to go through the roof.' People say things. They don't always mean harm by them and sometimes they actually believe them themselves, sometimes out of wishful thinking and sometimes because they think they know a movie will be successful. Sometimes they are right, sometimes not, but when you've been producing for a while you get the feel for when someone's lying or talking rubbish. Oliver wasn't bullshitting. He genuinely believed that the film was going to be massive and, I have to say, I thought so, too. This was the news that I had been hoping for. Gargantuan success, it seemed, was just around the corner.

With work completed on *The Magic Christian* Ringo returned to the recording studio to make what was to be the Beatles' last recorded LP, *Abbey Road*. It was an extraordinary album, and producer George Martin still claims it as one of their finest achievements. After the 'back to basics' approach that had been so problematic with the 'Get Back' project, the return to state-of-the-art studio production with George

Martin at the helm proved to be a much happier experience for all concerned.

The album, released in September 1969, was in some respects rather like a more disciplined version of the 'White Album'. In common with that LP, *Abbey Road* boasted an enormously accomplished range of musical styles. As with the 'White Album', each song was inscribed with the Beatles' unmistakable melodic signature, although *Abbey Road* was much slicker, with most of the second side segued into the ambitious medley with elaborate orchestrations and solos. It was as if the Beatles were responding to the critics who had argued that the four sides of the 'White Album' were too disjointed and scrappy. Even a devotee of that LP such as myself would have to concede that *Abbey Road* is a more polished and less erratic album. Although there is still a clear sense of individuality in terms of the song-writing contributions, the recording and the arrangements were much more of a group effort than any Beatles recording or release since *Sergeant Pepper*. Whether it is the finest of their albums is, however, a moot point. It certainly contained some convincing work and included two of George's finest songs, 'Something' and 'Here Comes the Sun', both of which have since become standards. The former, a love song to Pattie, was the first George Harrison song to be released as the A-side of a Beatles single and was later described by Frank Sinatra as 'the finest love song of the last fifty years'. 'Here Comes the Sun', which was, ironically, written at the height of the Beatles' business disagreements, remains one of the most uplifting pop songs ever written.[1]

Paul, John and Ringo also made first-class contributions, the latter providing another solo number (the country-inflected 'Octopus's Garden') and reaching new heights of excellence with his drumming, which is never less than inspired. John's powerful rockers 'Come Together' and 'I Want You' topped and tailed the first side of the LP, while his classically influenced 'Because' preceded the medley on the second side. His other contributions, 'Mean Mr Mustard' and 'Polythene Pam', were acerbic Liverpudlian character sketches, too lightweight to be recorded as full-length songs when they were demoed for the 'White Album' but perfect for the medley. *Abbey Road* represented a clear return to form for John in terms of his creative imput to the group.

Paul, who had arguably hit the peak of his songwriting abilities with the 'Get Back' sessions, was also on form for the album, with great songs and performances, including the blues of 'Oh Darling' and the children's song 'Maxwell's Silver Hammer', which the other Beatles hated. (Incidentally I supplied the anvil for the track from Twickenham Studios' props department.) Paul's greatest contribution, however, was undoubtedly his work on the medley, much of which he composed. Its final lyrical sentiments (in 'The End') neatly summarized the Beatles' optimistic philosophy of peaceful goodwill in a way that was partly glorious, partly heartbreaking and totally breathtaking. This was music made in aural widescreen, epic in its scope and astonishing in its execution. It was played with all the fervor and intensity of a group who knew that this was to be their last testament.

The LP was ecstatically received by critics and public on its release, and thirty years later it continues to be placed highly in 'greatest album' polls. The album sleeve, with its famous zebra-crossing photograph, is, together with the sleeve of *Sergeant Pepper's Lonely Hearts Club Band*, one of the most famous record covers of all time and one of the most enduring images of the sixties.[2]

Mid-December saw the British royal première of *The Magic Christian*, which took place at London's Kensington Odeon cinema. Once again it was a starry event. John appeared with Yoko dressed in a white suit and clutching a sandwich board that read 'Britain Murdered Hanratty'. By now he had practically disassociated himself from the rest of the Beatles, despite his outstanding imput to *Abbey Road*. By late 1969 he had turned into a kind of highbrow peacenik, mounting consciousness-raising events and happenings such as the famous 'bed-ins' in

Toronto and Amsterdam. His latest cause was James Hanratty, who had been hanged some six years earlier for a murder he may not have committed. John and Yoko also funded a documentary film called *Hanratty* designed to raise public awareness of the issue. The première was a great success and a fabulous time was had by all. I was very grateful for the support that John had given Ringo and the film, despite the fact that it was John's protest that grabbed the headlines in the following morning's newspapers.

After the Christmas and New Year holidays, the next phase in the promotion of *The Magic Christian* was the US première, which took place in Los Angeles on 29 January. We stayed at the elite Beverly Hills Hotel with Joe and Peta. Again, it was a very starry occasion, and Ringo and Maureen flew out to attend together with quite a few of the film's other stars.

I sat next to Yul Brynner, who leaned over to me saying, 'I hope this cross-dressing thing isn't going to mean the end of my career.'

'Don't worry,' I told him. 'If it is, you can always get leading lady parts!'

Afterwards Ringo suggested that a small group of us go to Las Vegas to see Elvis. The King was playing his comeback shows over at the International Hotel there, and Ringo and Maureen thought that while they were in the USA it would be fun to check them out. Ringo, of course, had met Elvis before. In 1965 the Beatles had visited him at his home at Bel Air when their US tour reached California. Despite the fact that they were initially uneasy about the meeting he and the Fab Four had got along splendidly, the group joining him for an impromptu jamming session. The Beatles had idolized Elvis above all their other American rock-and-roll heroes, John publicly stating that without him there would have been no Beatles. Anyway, Ringo and Maureen had decided that they were going to see his new show, so the next day Donna and I and Joe and Peta jetted off on the next leg of our American adventure.

On arriving in Las Vegas we had a couple of hours to spare before we were to meet for the cabaret, so Donna and I walked up the strip soaking in the atmosphere. We went to Circus Circus and, after an enjoyable dinner, were more than ready for the main event. Arriving at the show was an experience in itself. The Vegas International was one of the most extraordinary buildings on earth, its imposing grandeur at once unbearably gauche and jaw-droppingly impressive. A further treat awaited us. Word had gone round that one of the Beatles was bringing a party of friends and associates to the show and a special round table had been placed directly centre in front of the stage. No sooner had we sat down than the spotlight swung round to our table and announced our presence. Moments later we were told that Elvis would be glad to see us in the interval. We were thrilled and embarrassed in equal measure.

After a fantastic first set we were ushered backstage. Donna frantically looked around for something to ask the King to sign: in the end she had to settle for a couple of hotel menus from the table. We were taken into one of the dressing-rooms where we were asked to wait. Within moments Elvis arrived resplendent in a green brocade dressing-robe. We sat and made small talk for a few minutes, and he seemed genuinely pleased to see Ringo, despite rumours that he disapproved of the Beatles' lyrical references to drugs.

After a while he stood up to leave. 'It's been a pleasure to meet y'all, but I have to go finish changing.'

He shook hands all round, signed the menus, exchanged a few words with Ringo and was gone, swallowed up by an army of assistants and bodyguards. We hurried back to our table in time for the second half of the show.

The concert was undoubtedly the most professional solo performance by a singer I have ever seen. Elvis was slightly taller than I had expected but seemed to be in perfect shape physically, having recently made the famous comeback television special that had heralded his return to live performance. For the first half of the show he was dressed in a stunning body-hugging fine black leather catsuit open to

185

the waist and for the second half a similar outfit in white. Although his voice was as powerful as ever, what impressed me most was his stage-craft. It was fascinating to watch him work an audience at such close quarters, the way that he could bring such a variety of emotion to his performance, punctuating his delivery with expert timing and raising and lowering the intensity of the atmosphere at a stroke. He was, quite simply, the ultimate showman.

In my profession you don't get star-struck. You work with stars all the time, and, although some are remarkably talented and some are remarkably difficult and some are both in equal measure, you relate to them as people rather than the demi-gods that their publicity machine makes them out to be. But, I must admit, it was truly fantastic to meet Elvis backstage that night in Las Vegas. Not because he was necessarily more talented than many of the people that I have worked with but because his fame and iconic status in popular culture somehow placed him beyond conventional ideas of 'stardom'. This man, together with James Dean and Marilyn Monroe, was one of the most famous indi-viduals of the twentieth century. He didn't say anything profound. He didn't even pick up his guitar and sing to us. He didn't need to. He was Elvis. He was beyond fame.

After the show we parted company and went our separate ways for what was left of the night. Donna and I managed to take in the last half of a performance by Dean Martin (another highlight in itself!) and finally a late-night show by Ike and Tina Turner, before dropping into bed exhausted after a day we will never forget. In the morning it was as if the lights of a giant carousel had been turned off; apart from a background buzz of the 24-hour casinos, the rattle of the slot machines and the rustle of litter and losing tickets, the city streets seemed strangely quiet. Las Vegas never sleeps, but every now and then it does have a bit of a lie-down.

It had been truly memorable week, and we returned to the UK in excellent spirits. *The Magic Christian* was now going on general release, and, if the reception was anything as positive as the test screenings, we were about to become very, very rich. This, I thought, is as good as it gets. It cannot get better. I was right. It couldn't. And it didn't.

The Magic Christian performed disastrously at the box office, and I never made a bean out of the film. Why did it fail? I'm not entirely sure. There were probably a couple of contributory factors. To begin with, the film's release was delayed and its marketing and publicity were pretty poor because Commonwealth Films were going through financial problems. Secondly, and perhaps most important, was the fact that the critics, particularly in Britain, hated it.

I was naturally disappointed by the film's commercial failure but not devastated. The screenwriter William Goldman once famously said that in the film industry 'nobody knows anything'. He's right. As a producer, every film you make is based on a series of reasoned decisions about what you think an audience wants. There are obvious considerations and ingredients that are requisite factors in any commercial film's make-up: recognizable actors, a competent scriptwriter and director, clearly delineated genre and so on. But while you do your best to ensure that a film meets these various criteria you can never legislate against commercial failure because Goldman's observation is ultimately true: nobody really knows anything, although 'nobody knows everything' might be more accurate.

All movie producers are aware of this fundamental uncertainty from the off or discover it early on in their careers. In fact, I believe that it is, paradoxically, what drives us. Most producers are gamblers at heart. You have to be. If it were possible to make successful films by numbers, the job would not be remotely alluring.

For the record, though, I was pleased with the final cut of the picture and felt it was an entertaining meditation on the nature of human greed, avarice and materialism. I thought that Joe had made an excellent and stylish job of the direction and that Terry, Joe and Peter had, with a little help from John Cleese and Graham Chapman, produced an excellent script. Ringo, Peter and the rest of the cast performed well, the movie had a great soundtrack and there were a host of star cameos to add an extra touch of glamour to the proceedings. Actually I think it was partly the cameos that got us into trouble with critics, as I had the distinct feeling that this encouraged them to see the movie as a throwaway, a film with no real substance. Many, I think, reasoned that any picture with this many celebrities in it had to be frivolous and vacuous.

Perhaps, however, the film will receive critical and commercial reassessment one day. It certainly wouldn't surprise me, as it has happened on more than one occasion in my career, most famously with Michael Cimino's epic western *Heaven's Gate*, which I part-produced some ten years later. The film, as all movie buffs know, was a notorious critical and commercial failure on its release but has since come to be regarded as a classic of its genre. Partly this may have been because the film was later rereleased with more of its original footage, making it much more comprehensible, and partly it is due to the fact that the rediscovery of neglected artworks is the lifeblood of the critical establishment. Without this, entire publications would cease to exist. Without it, musicians of the calibre of Tim Buckley and Nick Drake would have been heard by hardly anyone and films such as *Night of the Hunter* would have been seen only by a handful of lucky viewers. Sometimes, however, you can't help feeling like screaming, 'Where the hell were you when the bloody thing came out?'

13

Sorry, Wrong Number

THE MAGIC CHRISTIAN loosely coincided with the end of my association with the Beatles. I kept in touch with developments in the immediate aftermath of the film, but I never returned officially to Apple as Director of Films, Publicity or anything else. The band were in the advanced stages of their final break-up by early 1970. I was, however, astonished to discover that finally, some fifteen months after the cameras first turned over, the 'Get Back' project, now renamed *Let It Be*, was going to see the light of day, both in the cinemas and in the record shops.

The film turned out to be a great deal more rewarding than the album. Unable to agree on either of the mixes made by Glyn Johns, Klein had drafted in Phil Spector to perform a salvage job on the tapes without Paul's knowledge. The resulting LP, with its heavily contrived overdubs of choirs and strings, was something of a perversion of the original 'live' premise and, in my opinion, not in the same league as either of the Glyn Johns mixes.

John publicly defended Spector's work, claiming that he had made something out of the 'biggest load of badly recorded shit', while Paul felt completely betrayed, both personally and musically. He was particularly dismayed at what he saw as the destruction of 'The Long and Winding Road'. Spector's version of the song, with its saccharine strings and 'heavenly choir' backing vocals, was later mentioned in Paul's legal disputes with the other Beatles as an example of their artistic animosity. Unsurprisingly, while George and John continued to work with Spector throughout the early seventies (among others he co-produced George's *All Things Must Pass* and John's *Plastic Ono Band* and *Imagine* albums) *Let It Be* marked the beginning and end of his creative association with Paul. Worse still, the LP release also became the subject of a great deal of internal disagreement when Paul grew angry that the release of the soundtrack album would delay that of his own solo project, *McCartney*. A fearsome row broke out between Paul and the others, who maintained that the release date could not be changed because Allen Klein had arranged with United Artists for the soundtrack LP to coincide with the release of the film. In the end Paul got his way, but it was the last straw.

The other three members of the band had threatened to quit the group: Ringo had walked out for two weeks during the recording of the 'White Album' and George had left during the 'Get Back' sessions. Both of these incidents turned out to be little more than minor flare-ups, although they were unquestionably an indication of the disintegration of the group's personal and artistic harmony. The most serious blow to the future of the Beatles had come in September 1969, when John had announced to the other members of the group that he had had enough and was leaving. He was persuaded to keep this quiet, as an open announcement at that stage would have greatly harmed Klein's record royalty negotiations. Ironically, it was Paul, the one who had so desperately tried to keep the Beatles together, who was to announce the group's demise. Much to John's chagrin, on 10 April 1970 Paul became the first to state publicly that he wished to break free of the band and that he saw no future in the Lennon–McCartney songwriting partnership. This information, gleaned from a heavily contrived 'interview', was included in review copies of the new *McCartney* LP and effectively meant that the Beatles, the most successful pop group of all time, had ceased to exist.

The *Let It Be* movie was premièred in the USA in May 1970. None of the former Beatles attended and neither did I. Although I effectively produced the film, I gave my production credit to Neil, who at that time was keen to get into film production. Credits have never meant that much to me anyway, and I was happy to help his career. Not that he needed any assistance, as it turned out. Indeed he had toiled very hard on the production of the film, working, as ever, as a key mediator between the Beatles and always making sure that things ran as smoothly as possible in very difficult circumstances.

Let It Be did, of course, evolve into a fascinating film, but it is fascinating mainly because what you are seeing is four remarkable characters interacting with each other. There is no real shape to the finished movie and, although the impromptu rooftop concert provided a fitting end to the proceedings, I can't help but think of some of the ideas that got away. That said, the film benefits from its sparseness, the spontaneity and simplicity of the concert giving it an authenticity that a more heavily contrived film sequence might possibly have spoiled.

Despite the lack of personal promotion and some fairly scathing reviews, the film performed well commercially and won the Beatles an Oscar for best score. It must be admitted that the film's timing was fortuitous. Although fascination with the Beatles continued throughout the sixties, I don't think that a documentary would have been as much of a commercial success if it had been released midway through the group's career. Conversely, another fictional movie would not have been as successful at this point either. After all, the stories, scandals and speculation which had been mounting in the media from 1968 and which came to a head with the announcement of the split greatly enhanced *Let It Be*'s appeal. Audiences wanted to know how these people, about whom they had heard and read so much, interacted with each other in real life. Were they really all enemies? Did they really have arguments? And if that were the case, what were the rehearsals like? Although *Let It Be* didn't provide the answers to all of these questions, it certainly presented a pretty accurate record of the misery of the Twickenham sessions, and with its inclusion of the famous argument between George and Paul, had a compelling fly-on-the-wall quality rare in pop films before or since. Together with the Maysles

191

brothers' documentary of the group's first American visit, *Yeah, Yeah, Yeah!* (also known as *What's Happening: The Beatles in the USA*), *Let It Be* is one of the very few pieces of extended 'behind the scenes' documentary footage of the group in existence, which is surprising given their huge popularity and the sheer volume of television and film footage in which they featured.

Like the rest of the world, I was saddened by the Beatles' break-up. Although I had watched the disintegration of the band from a privileged position and was therefore unsurprised at the final split, it was still genuinely depressing when it came. As well as the realization that there would be no more music from the Beatles as a group, it was a terrible shame that it ended in such an ugly way. It was a great irony that a national institution whose message had been one of universal love and goodwill should part on such bitter terms and that in the end the Beatles were unable to practise the ideals of peace and harmony to which they aspired. Relations were particularly strained between John and Paul. The former was bitterly unhappy because, to all the world, it seemed as though Paul had broken up the band that he still regarded as predominantly 'his', despite the fact that it was really Paul who had been the key player in the group's activities for the last three years. John felt that Paul had stolen his thunder and was angry at what he saw as his 'selfishness' over the release of *McCartney*. For his part, Paul was desperately unhappy with Allen Klein and wanted out of Apple and the Beatles' partnership. The problem was that dissolving the partnership would have meant an enormous tax bill for each of them, and although Paul wanted to get out the others weren't so keen. In the weeks that followed the news of his departure Paul went through a dreadful crisis of conscience. He came to the terrible realization that the only way that he could free himself from his association with Klein was by taking the other three Beatles to court to break up the partnership. In the end, of course, he did just that. Following a painful court case that began in January 1971 (during which many of the Beatles artistic and personal tensions were aired publicly), it was finally ruled that the Beatles' earnings go to a caretaker receiver until the complex financial and legal dissolution of their partnership could be resolved.

The end of the Beatles effectively heralded the end of Britain as a locus of pop culture. And while the rise of punk in the seventies once again focused attention on the British scene, to some the movement now seems more important as a cultural moment than for the music it produced. That said, it was possibly the last moment in pop that had any kind of genuine inspiration or articulated an important social message. Punk, for all its eventual commercialization, challenged its audience, which is a great deal more than one can say about current mainstream pop which, some would argue, has been in decline since the early seventies.

Part of this is because the Beatles – and the more talented of their contemporaries – existed in a period when the mechanics of the modern popular music industry were still in their infancy, before the cynicism of marketing strategies had rendered the concept of experimentation an irritating and potentially destructive nuisance. While buoyant economically, the contemporary mainstream British pop music scene has never been in a worse state in terms of genuine innovation, with less variation than at any point in its history.

Much of this is to do with the juvenilization of the singles market, which now seems hell-bent on processing dance-oriented karaoke boy and girl groups *ad infinitum*, like offal from some hellish sausage machine. Of course, the manufacture and manipulation of image is as old as the music industry itself. However, the current preoccupation with inane cover versions, slick choreography and high-concept corporate branding (in other words, everything apart from original musical content) has never been greater than now. It is a sad indictment of pop's current sterility that we seem to have returned to a climate not dissimilar to that which existed in the very late fifties and early sixties in Britain, a time when the raw sexuality and potentially subversive power of rock and roll degenerated into bland pretty-boy sterility and insipid balladeering.

Following the Beatles' split, I saw little of them and returned to film production, making movies such as *The Offence* (1973) and *Heaven's Gate* (1980). I also renewed my partnership with Richard Lester on several movies in the seventies, including *Juggernaut* (1974), *Royal Flash* (1975), *Robin and Marian* (1976) and *Cuba* (1979). Yet in the immediate aftermath of the break-up Donna and I were to feel the full force of the Beatles' influence in a way that we never had when they were together.

One evening in March 1970 we were having a quiet night in at our house in St George's Square when the telephone rang.

Donna went to answer it. 'Hello?'

There was a short silence before a deep male voice with an American accent said, 'We know your name and now we've got your number.' Straight away the caller hung up.

The next day I was over at Twickenham studios when a repeat call was made in the late afternoon at the house. This was pretty worrying. We had had one or two nuisance calls in the past but never anything like this. It seemed extremely sinister, and as the recipient of the calls Donna was particularly concerned for our safety. The words sounded like some kind of threat.

Over the next three days similar calls were received from a variety of different callers, mostly American males, and we began to get very anxious indeed. Who were these people, and what did they want? London was by no means a risk-free city in which to live, albeit less violent than many American ones. That weekend I was home, and we agreed I would take all the incoming calls.

Sure enough, there was another call, but this time I managed to keep the man on the line. It wasn't easy to communicate with him, because as well as being pretty inarticulate he was also, by his own admission, very stoned. In the end, however, it all began to fall into place.

It turned out that he was calling from Philadelphia, where he worked in a candle factory. He had heard my name mentioned on the B-side of the Beatles' last UK single, 'You Know My Name (Look Up the Number)', and done just that, getting my number from international directory enquiries.

As he droned on, I recalled that almost a year earlier, on 2 May 1969, Ringo and Peter Sellers had thrown an informal surprise party at Twickenham with the *Magic Christian* cast and crew to celebrate my birthday. The proceedings had been pretty rowdy, and there was a great deal of noise, but midway through the proceedings Ringo played me a tape of the song, which – it turned out – the Beatles had just finished recording. Although amused by it I was immersed in the production of the film and quickly forgot about it. At the time I thought it was just a little comedy number they had composed for my birthday. I certainly didn't think the group would release it commercially. And I was almost right, since the track went unreleased for some eleven months after it was recorded, eventually surfacing as one of the oddest B-sides in pop history.

At the time of the mystery calls I had not heard the final version of the finished record, which had been released only a few days earlier. The song, which is lyrically little more than a mantra of the title, included some spoken references to a Denis O'Bell! The candle-maker from Philadelphia knew, presumably from reading about the Beatles, that this was a reference to yours truly.[1] Had my name been 'Harris' or 'Jones' it would have been impossible for him to track me down, but since there were only two 'O'Dells' in the London telephone directory at the time his task had not been difficult.

When the caller, who was clearly somewhat unhinged and certainly very high, explained himself it all made a kind of crazy sense within the confines of this deranged fan's obsessive and unbalanced mind. He had interpreted the song as an invitation from me to make contact. He was calling because, he said, he and his commune wanted to come to live with us.

Talking to him took a load off our minds, for, although he was pretty far gone, he didn't sound aggressive or threatening. I told him that we weren't taking lodgers, and the phone calls stopped. So that was that. Or so we thought.

A couple of weeks later we were out for the day when Betty, our housekeeper, went to answer the doorbell. She opened it and standing in the doorway were eight rather bedraggled-looking hippies. They had come from the candle factory in Philadelphia to live with us. Fortunately Betty had the presence of mind to tell them we didn't live in the house any more, and they left. That was the last that was seen of them. Good job, too. While in all probability they were simply a bunch of harmless hippies, the combination of drugs and obsessive fan worship is something that I found extremely disconcerting, particularly since the horror of the Manson murders, which were still fresh in the public consciousness.

But it was marvellous to think that the Beatles decided to use my name in a song, however bizarre the consequences. Strangely enough, Paul has since said that it is probably his favourite Beatles track, maintaining that its recording, which took place over a two-year period, was the most enjoyable of the group's career. Considering that it is probably the oddest, most obscure track they ever recorded, that seems quite a statement, but then the Beatles were nothing if not contrary. Whatever, it is a wonderful and permanent memento of the strangest, most exhilarating chapter of my life.

Epilogue
Some Time in New York City

IN SPRING 1981 I was having lunch in Gino's, the celebrity New York restaurant not far from the Dakota building where in December the year before John Lennon had been assassinated. Together with the rest of the world I was immensely saddened by his death and angered by the sheer senselessness of it all. Like many of the people who had known John well in the sixties I had lost contact with him in the seventies but was happy to see him make the 1980 comeback that was cut so tragically short. His death robbed the world of a poet, musician, artist, film-maker, actor and peace campaigner whose violent murder was riddled with bitter irony.

John's murder was unusual in that he was the victim of a celebrity stalker but less unusual in that thousands of Americans live and die by the gun. Bemoaning the final, irrevocable loss of the Beatles is trivial and selfish in the circumstances, for this sobering thought is infinitely more devastating than the breaking up of a pop group or the loss of a body of work that John never got to produce. The real tragedies are the human ones: the relationship he never got to have with his children, the devastation it inflicted on his wife and friends, the physical pain of bleeding to death in the back of an ambulance.

In the wake of his murder, the lionization of John has increased his iconic status (something that he genuinely never wanted), and this has had the unfortunate effect of desensitizing us to those very human qualities which made him an icon in the first place.

*

197

My lunch was with my friend Louis J. Nicastro and some business associates. We were midway through our meal when, to my great surprise, Salvatore, the head waiter, ushered Yoko and a group of her friends into the restaurant. I hadn't seen her for many years, but I looked over at her and she smiled in recognition. This was a very different Yoko to the one I remembered from the Apple years. She was immaculately turned out, a far cry from her bohemian days in London. After lunch I went across to her and over a cup of coffee offered my sympathies and condolences and told her how sorry I had been about John's death. She was very gracious, telling me that John had often talked fondly about me when he was reminiscing about the old days. This was both moving and heartening, since, although my relationship with John had always been good, there had been one or two tense moments between us towards the end of our association.

Once in the late sixties he had approached me about getting a mainstream distribution deal for an avant-garde film he had made with Yoko called *Smile*. The movie, made in 1968, featuring a one-hour close-up shot of John smiling in ultra-slow motion, would have been utterly impossible to get on to the major circuits, and I told him so. I'm afraid to say that I may have been rather short with him about it. Anyway he was not a happy man – and John did not always take kindly to being told no. I didn't hear from him for several days after that little run-in and was saddened to think that our friendship, which I valued dearly, may have come to an end.

A few more days passed, and I heard nothing. Then, arriving at the office late one afternoon, I found a huge piece of white card on my desk. It was accompanied by one of John's famous line-drawing caricatures of himself. In the centre of the card, in black biro, was a tiny dot. Above the dot, in John's hand, was a scrawled message.

'I was here, where were you?' it said.

Notes

Chapter 1: Meet the Beatles

1. *The Mouse on the Moon* was the sequel to an earlier comedy, *The Mouse That Roared* (1959), which had starred Peter Sellers. The film, very much in the Ealing comedy tradition (although not an Ealing picture), was directed by Jack Arnold.

2. One reason for the authenticity of Owen's screenplay is the fact that he had personally observed the group at close quarters over a three-day period in November 1963, accompanying them on a trip to play in Dublin and Belfast. This had been organized by Walter Shenson to help Owen in his research.

3. Fred had been a steward on an ocean liner and until 1964 had not been seen by John since he was five years old. He was working as a kitchen hand at a London hotel when he was reunited with his son. He later gained minor celebrity status when his novelty record, 'That's My Life', was issued shortly afterwards.

Chapter 2: How the War Was Won

1. For John's fascinating insights and opinions of the Beatles songs he composed, the reader is directed towards Jan Wenner's *Lennon Remembers* (Penguin, Harmondsworth, 1973) and David Sheff's and G. Barry Olson's *Playboy Interviews with John Lennon* (New English Library, Sevenoaks, 1982). Both books contain virtual song-by-song comments and opinions by Lennon on the inspiration and execution of his work as a Beatle.

Chapter 3: Long Hot Summer

1. Apart from the record-sleeve designs of the period, nowhere is the Beatles'

change of image better displayed than in Richard Avedon's extraordinary psychedelic portraits from early 1968. Originally used for a contemporary poster design, the images were more recently utilized by Apple for the rear cover of the hugely popular compilation of the Beatles' hits, *One*.

2. Although all of the Beatles actively supported underground publications such as *International Times* and *Oz* throughout the late sixties, both John and Paul were particularly enthusiastic in this respect. As well as contributing financially, Paul helped his friend Barry Miles with an exclusive first issue interview for *IT*, and John gave financial and vocal support to *Oz*, for which he produced the track 'God Save Oz' in 1971. An interesting discussion of the Beatles' relationship with the underground press can be found in Miles's *Many Years from Now* (Secker and Warburg, London, 1997).

3. Most famously, of course, it was Brian who had to fire Pete Best from the group when the Beatles were on the threshold of fame. This must have been a desperately difficult task and one which, according to virtually all accounts, the Beatles themselves could not bring themselves to do face to face. There have, of course, been many accounts of Brian's life and career. The most comprehensive is probably Ray Coleman's biography, *Brian Epstein: The Man Who Made the Beatles* (Penguin, Harmondsworth, 1988).

4. In this sense, Brian's vision matched that of the Beatles themselves, who were arguably the first rock group to overcome the transient nature of pop culture. Certainly few managers in pop history have placed as much confidence in the ability of their artists to evolve and change artistically while remaining successful commercially.

Chapter 4: The Mystery Trip

1. Ken Kesey's involvement with Apple is discussed in some depth in Richard Dilello's *The Longest Cocktail Party* (Charisma, London, 1972).

2. Paul also made an appearance on *The Frost Programme* on 27 December in which he defended the film against the tirade of bad reviews it had received the previous day.

Chapter 5: Gurus, Gods and Gollum

1. The film was the first British animated feature since the cartoon version of George Orwell's political parable *Animal Farm* in 1954.

2. Paul made a number of controversial comments relating to LSD in summer 1967, the most famous of which appeared in *Life* magazine in the USA and *Queen* magazine in the UK. Pressed by reporters about his drug use, Paul admitted to having taken hallucinogenics, saying that 'we only use one-tenth of our brain. Just think of what we could accomplish if we could only tap that hidden part. If the politicians would take LSD, there wouldn't be any more war, or poverty or famine.' The comments, predictably, created an enormous furore in the tabloid press, echoing the controversy of John's notorious 'we're bigger than Jesus' comments from the previous year.
3. The promos shot that day comprised several versions of five different songs. These were 'Help!', 'Daytripper', 'We Can Work It Out', 'I Feel Fine' and 'Ticket to Ride'.

Chapter 6: Twilight of the Gods

1. Beatles mythology offers several versions of who was supposedly earmarked for which character in the book. None of them, to the best of my knowledge, are correct. Although John had plans to play Gandalf, Paul, George and Ringo never settled on definitive roles for themselves during these discussions.

Chapter 7: The Big Apple

1. Originally released in 1968 and produced by Graham Nash, the LP was reissued on CD in the late nineties.

Chapter 8: Another Day at the Office

1. He had also attained experience of live studio recordings as a director of the famed sixties pop show *Ready Steady Go!* The Beatles appeared several times on the show between 1963 and 1965, so they knew Michael well by the time they came to make the 'Hey Jude'/'Revolution' promos.
2. A firsthand account of this little stunt can be found in Richard Dilello's *The Longest Cocktail Party*.

Chapter 9: Unhappy New Year

1. Much attention has been given to 'While My Guitar Gently Weeps', although, for my money, 'Long, Long, Long' is his most resonant ballad.
2. He was eventually coaxed back into the fold to find that the others had

garlanded his drums with flowers. During his absence Paul, the most versatile instrumentalist in the group, drummed on 'Dear Prudence' and 'Back in the USSR'.

3. In the final part of the *Beatles Anthology* documentary series Paul discusses this policy at some length, maintaining that it possibly accentuated the business difficulties concerning the running of Apple.

4. The others, of course, were 'Lady Madonna', 'Get Back' and 'Let It Be'.

5. I remember, for example, taking film director Franco Zeffirelli to one session at Abbey Road.

Chapter 10: We Can't Work It Out

1. See Mark Lewisohn's *Complete Beatles Recording Sessions* (Hamlyn, London, 1989) for a full discussion of Alex's 'studio'.

2. The songs performed on the rooftop included versions of 'Get Back', 'Don't Let Me Down', 'I've Got a Feeling', 'One After 909' and 'Dig a Pony'.

3. Interestingly, one of the highpoints of Paul's post-Beatles career, the *Band on the Run* LP, was also produced in difficult circumstances. It was recorded in a half-built studio in Lagos following the sudden departure of two former members of Wings.

Chapter 11: Carry On Till Tomorrow

1. Terry co-wrote the screenplay to this, the archetypal late-sixties road movie, with the film's stars Peter Fonda and Dennis Hopper. Fonda and Hopper also produced and directed respectively.

2. Somebody may eventually write a book on the close connections between the Beatles and Monty Python, as after the band's split there were many collaborations between ex-Beatles and Pythons. Most famously, George Harrison's Handmade Films was formed to finance the Pythons' seminal picture *The Life of Brian* in 1979.

Chapter 12: A Taste of Honey

1. The song was written in Eric Clapton's garden. Although it was recorded in a far more productive atmosphere than the *Let It Be* sessions, it was completed without any contribution from John. A few days before its recording he was involved in a motor accident in Scotland and was hospitalized

with Yoko and her daughter Kyoko until the day before the recording session took place.

2. Ironically for such an enduring image, the cover came about partly as a result of the Beatles' apathy. One of the original ideas was that the album should be called *Everest* and the group would fly over to the Himalayas to pose in front of the mountain. Nobody could be bothered, however, and it was decided that the album simply be named after the studio the Beatles had made so famous. The front cover picture, shot by photographer Ian Macmillan, was based on a sketch devised by Paul and proved a far easier option.

Chapter 13: Sorry, Wrong Number

1. Although not released until 1970, work commenced on the song in May 1967 while the Beatles were recording a clutch of tracks that would eventually find their way on to soundtrack releases for *Yellow Submarine* and *Magical Mystery Tour*. It featured Rolling Stone Brian Jones on sax and sound-effects generated by Mal Evans, who was instructed by John and Paul to shovel gravel in time to the song! Originally over six minutes long, the recording was mooted as one side of a single for the Plastic Ono Band (the other being John and Yoko's 'What's the New Mary Jane?'). This never happened, however, and a shorter version was released as the B-side of 'Let It Be'. The full-length version was finally issued on the second part of the *Beatles Anthology* series.

Twenty Recommended Books on the Beatles

Despite the critical comments in the introduction to this book, it has to be acknowledged that the Beatles have inspired some fascinating writing. I would like to share with you my alphabetical list of those books that I have particularly enjoyed for various different reasons over the years, some of which have also proven to be useful sources of information in the preparation of this volume. You will probably be familiar with many of them. This is not intended to be a comprehensive list. Hundreds of books have been written about the band, many of which have something to recommend them, and I have omitted reference books and diary accounts. This means that Mark Lewisohn's *Complete Beatles Chronicle* and Barry Miles's *The Beatles: An Illustrated Diary* do not appear below, despite the fact that they are both valuable sources of information and, in the case of the Lewisohn book, the most impressive large-scale piece of research on the group ever undertaken.

Badman, Keith, *The Beatles Off the Record* (Omnibus, London, 2000). With a brief introduction by Hunter Davies, this exhaustive labour of love comprises transcript extracts from long-lost sixties interviews. Without the concessions to nostalgia and romanticism, *Off the Record* is a kind of gritty cousin to the official *Beatles Anthology* and no worse for it. One of the most interesting and comprehensive archival works to appear in recent years.

Beatles, *The Beatles Anthology* (Cassell, London, 2000). Very much an 'official' history, *The Beatles Anthology* is required reading. Designed in collaboration with Genesis Publications, a company that specializes in limited editions, it is also the most sumptuously produced mass-market book on popular music to appear in Britain for many years.

Braun, Michael, *Love Me Do* (Penguin, Harmondsworth, 1964). The earliest serious study of the Beatles, Braun's account of the early days of Beatlemania remains as readable today as it was in 1964. Quite possibly the most underrated volume on the group ever produced.

Brown, Peter and Steven Gaines, *The Love You Make* (Pan, London, 1984). Rather over-sensational in style and a little too concerned with dishing the dirt, this is nevertheless a diverting book from a man who was genuinely part of the 'inner circle'.

Davies, Hunter, *The Beatles* (Mayflower, London, 1969). Up until the *Anthology*, this was the only official authorized book on the group. It has dated surprisingly well and has some fascinating firsthand observations of John and Paul composing 'With a Little Help from My Friends' in 1967.

Dilello, Richard, *The Longest Cocktail Party* (Charisma, London, 1972). Amusing account of the early history of Apple, recently reissued by Mojo Books.

Evans, Mike, *The Art of the Beatles* (Anthony Blond, London, 1984). Long out-of-print account of the Beatles' influence on pop art. Beautifully illustrated and comprehensive.

Inglis, Ian (editor), *The Beatles, Popular Music and Society* (Macmillan, London, 2000). Rather hit and miss in places, this collection of academic articles on various aspects of the Beatles' career still makes rewarding reading.

Kozinn, Alan, *The Beatles* (Phaidon, London, 1995). Although perhaps slightly less penetrating than Ian MacDonald's book below, this is still a useful analytical work.

MacDonald, Ian, *Revolution in the Head: The Beatles' Records and the Sixties* (Fourth Estate, London, 1994). A remarkable sustained analysis of the Beatles' music.

Martin, George with Jeremy Hornsby, *All You Need Is Ears* (St Martin's

Press, New York, 1979). This is a charming and enlightening account of the great producer's work with the Beatles and other artists.

McCabe, Peter and Robert Schonfeld, *Apple to the Core* (Pocket Books, Ontario, 1972). Although I don't agree with some of the points that this account makes, this is an entertaining read which benefits from some exclusive interviews.

Melly, George, *Revolt into Style* (Allen Lane, Harmondsworth, 1970). Not a Beatles book *per se*, although the group do feature heavily in this masterful deconstruction of sixties pop culture; hence its inclusion in this list.

Miles, Barry, *Many Years from Now* (Secker and Warburg, London, 1997). Although criticized at the time for presenting a jaundiced view of John's contribution to the Beatles, this contains some interesting revelations from Paul, who gave Miles a series of exhaustive and detailed interviews for this account of his life and career as a Beatle.

Neaverson, Bob, *The Beatles Movies* (Cassell, London, 1997). The first critical history of the Beatles' films. Includes analyses of the films and insights from actors and directors such as Richard Lester, Joe McGrath and Victor Spinetti.

Sheff, David and G. Barry Golson, *The Playboy Interviews with John Lennon and Yoko Ono* (New English Library, Sevenoaks, 1982). Published after Lennon's death, these 1980 interview transcripts find John in a reflective and relaxed frame of mind. As with Jan Wenner's book below, there are some revealing and at times ridiculously self-deprecating accounts of his songs.

Sulphy, Doug and Ray Schweighardt, *Get Back: The Beatles' 'Let It Be' Disaster* (Helter Skelter, London, 1998). Fascinating blow-by-blow description of the *Let It Be* tapes. One of those books that works against all expectations; despite the minutiae of detail it frequently makes riveting reading.

Taylor, Derek, *It Was Twenty Years Ago Today* (Bantam, London, 1987). Written by the Beatles' press agent, this is, despite its title, like George Melly's *Revolt into Style*, more of a general study of sixties youth culture than a book purely on the Beatles. Beautifully written, as you might expect.

Walker, Alexander, *Hollywood, England* (Harrap, London, 1986). Not a Beatles book at all, this account of sixties British cinema does, however, contain useful information on the making of *A Hard Day's Night*.

Wenner, Jan, *Lennon Remembers* (Penguin, Harmondsworth, 1973). This contains sustained interview footage of John in angry Beatle-bashing mode. Aggressive and exceptionally uncharitable in places, he tried at one point to block the book's publication. However, his rapier wit, revealing insights and frequently painful honesty make this a completely irresistible read.

The Films of Denis O'Dell

As Assistant Director

On Approval (1942), directed by Brian Desmond Hurst/Clive Brook/Sydney Box, starring Clive Brook, Googie Withers, Beatrice Lillie

The Demi-Paradise (1943), directed by Anthony Asquith, starring Laurence Olivier, Penelope Dudley Ward

The Lamp Still Burns (1943), directed by Maurice Elvey, starring Stewart Granger, Rosamund John

So Evil My Love (1943), directed by Lewis Allen, starring Ray Milland, Ann Todd

So Well Remembered (1947), directed by Edward Dmytryk, starring John Mills

Woman Hater (1948), directed by Terence Young, starring Stewart Granger, Edwinge Feuillière

Trottie True (1949), directed by Brian Desmond Hurst, starring Jean Kent, Bill Owen, James Donald

The Perfect Woman (1949), directed by Terence Young, starring Patricia Roc, Nigel Patrick

The Reluctant Widow (1950), directed by Bernard Knowles, starring Jean Kent, Guy Rolfe

They Were Not Divided (1951), directed by Terence Young, starring Ralph Clanton, Edward Underdown, Helen Cherry

Valley of the Eagles (1951), directed by Terence Young, starring Nadia Gray, Jack Warner

Tom Brown's Schooldays (1951), directed by Gordon Parry, starring Robert Newton, John Howard Davies, James Hayter

Scrooge (1951), directed by Brian Desmond Hurst, starring Alastair Sim, Kathleen Harrison, George Cole

Emergency Call (1952), directed by Lewis Gilbert, starring Jack Warner, Sidney Tatler, Freddie Mills

Mother Riley Meets the Vampire (1952), directed by John Gilling, starring Arthur Lucan, Bela Lugosi

The Pickwick Papers (1952), directed by Noel Langley, starring James Hayter, James Donald, Nigel Patrick

The Tall Headlines (1952), directed by Terence Young, starring Michael Denison, Dulcie Gray

Grand National Night (1953), directed by Bob McNaught, starring Nigel Patrick, Moira Lister

Svengali (1954), directed by Noel Langley, starring Hildegarde Neff, Donald Wolfit

Dance Little Lady (1954), directed by Val Guest, starring Mandy Miller, Mai Zetterling

That Lady (1955), directed by Terence Young, starring Olivia de Havilland, Gilbert Roland, Paul Scofield

The Prisoner (1955), directed by Peter Glenville, starring Jack Hawkins, Alec Guinness

The Scamp (1956), directed by Wolf Rilla, starring Terence Morgan, Richard Attenborough

It's a Wonderful World (1956), directed by Val Guest, starring Mylene Demongeot, Terence Morgan

Carry On Admiral (1957: Writer/Producer), directed by Val Guest, starring David Tomlinson, Peggy Cummins

Tread Softly Stranger (1958: Writer/Producer), directed by Gordon Parry, starring Diana Dors, Terence Morgan, George Baker

Sea of Sand (1958: Second Unit Director), directed by Guy Green, starring Richard Attenborough, John Gregson

As Producer/Associate Producer

Rendezvous (1958–60, TV), various directors, starring Charles Drake, Peter O'Toole, Mel Ferrer, Gladys Cooper, Patricia Neal

A Midsummer Night's Dream (1961), directed by Peter Hall, starring Charles Laughton, Mary Ure

Playboy of the Western World (1962), directed by Brian Desmond Hurst, starring Siobhan McKenna, Gary Redmond

The Long Ships (1963), directed by Jack Cardiff, starring Richard Widmark, Sidney Poitier, Robert Shaw, Russ Tamblyn

A Hard Day's Night (1964), directed by Richard Lester, starring the Beatles, Wilfred Brambell, Norman Rossington, Victor Spinetti

The Bedford Incident (1965), directed by James B. Harris, starring Richard Widmark, Sidney Poitier

How I Won the War (1966), directed by Richard Lester, starring John Lennon, Michael Crawford

The Deadly Affair (1966), directed by Sydney Lumet, starring James Mason, Simone Signoret, Maximillian Schell

Kiss the Girls and Make Them Die (1966), directed by Harry Levin/Arduino Maiuri, starring Michael Connors, Raf Vallone, Dorothy Provine

Petulia (1967), directed by Richard Lester, starring George C. Scott, Julie Christie, Richard Chamberlain

Magical Mystery Tour (1967), directed by and starring the Beatles, Victor Spinetti, Ivor Cutler

Let It Be (1969), directed by Michael Lindsay-Hogg, starring the Beatles

The Magic Christian (1969), directed by Joe McGrath, starring Ringo Starr, Peter Sellers, Raquel Welch, Yul Brynner, Christopher Lee, Roman Polanski

The Offence (1973), directed by Sydney Lumet, starring Sean Connery, Ian Bannen, Trevor Howard

Juggernaut (1974), directed by Richard Lester, starring Richard Harris, Omar Sharif, Shirley Knight, Anthony Hopkins

Royal Flash (1975), directed by Richard Lester, starring Malcolm McDowell, Alan Bates, Oliver Reed, Britt Ekland, Florinda Bolkan

Robin and Marian (1976), directed by Richard Lester, starring Sean Connery, Audrey Hepburn, Robert Shaw, Richard Harris, Ronnie Barker

The Ritz (1976), directed by Richard Lester, starring Rita Moreno, F. Murray Abraham, Jack Weston

Cuba (1979), directed by Richard Lester, starring Sean Connery, Jack Weston, Brooke Adams

Heaven's Gate (1980), directed by Michael Cimino, starring Kris Kristofferson, Jeff Bridges, John Hurt, Isabelle Huppert

Index